NOLO® Products & Services

Books & Software

Get in-depth information. Nolo publishes hundreds of great books and software programs for consumers and business owners. Order a copy—or download an ebook version instantly—at Nolo.com.

Legal Encyclopedia

Free at Nolo.com. Here are more than 1,400 free articles and answers to common questions about everyday legal issues including wills, bankruptcy, small business formation, divorce, patents, employment and much more.

Plain-English Legal Dictionary

Free at Nolo.com. Stumped by jargon? Look it up in America's most up-to-date source for definitions of legal terms.

Online Legal Documents

Create documents at your computer. Go to Nolo.com to make a will or living trust, form an LLC or corporation or obtain a trademark or provisional patent. For simpler matters, download one of our hundreds of high-quality legal forms, including bills of sale, promissory notes, nondisclosure agreements and many more.

Lawyer Directory

Find an attorney at Nolo.com. Nolo's consumer-friendly lawyer directory provides in-depth profiles of lawyers all over America. From fees and experience to legal philosophy, education and special expertise, you'll find all the information you need to pick the right lawyer. Every lawyer listed has pledged to work diligently and respectfully with clients.

Free Legal Updates

Keep up to date. Check for free updates at Nolo.com. Under "Products," find this book and click "Legal Updates." You can also sign up for our free e-newsletters at Nolo.com/newsletters.

NOLO® The Trusted Name
(but don't take our word for it)

4th edition

LLC or Corporation?

How to Choose the Right Form for Your Business

by Attorney Anthony Mancuso

Fourth Edition	JANUARY 2011
Editor	RICHARD STIM
Cover Design	SUSAN PUTNEY
Production	MARGARET LIVINGSTON
Proofreading	ELAINE MERRILL
Index	SONGBIRD INDEXING
Printing	DELTA PRINTING SOLUTIONS, INC.

Mancuso, Anthony.
 LLC or corporation? : how to choose the right form for your business / by Anthony Mancuso. -- 4th ed.
  p. cm.
 Includes index.
 Summary: "Presents information needed to help entrepreneurs choose the appropriate business entity (limited liability company or corporation) for their companies. The 4th edition is updated to cover changes in tax and business law"--Provided by publisher.
 ISBN-13: 978-1-4133-1282-9 (pbk.)
 ISBN-10: 1-4133-1282-9 (pbk.)
 ISBN-13: 978-1-4133-1298-0 (e-book)
 ISBN-10: 1-4133-1298-5 (e-book)
 1. Private companies--United States--Popular works. I. Title.
 KF1380.M364 2010
 346.73'0668--dc22

                    2010021164

Please note

We believe accurate, plain-English legal information should help you solve many of your own legal problems. But this text is not a substitute for personalized advice from a knowledgeable lawyer. If you want the help of a trained professional—and we'll always point out situations in which we think that's a good idea—consult an attorney licensed to practice in your state.

Acknowledgments

Thanks to Rich Stim, my editor. As always, thanks to the hard-working Nolo staff for helping make this book a reality.

Table of Contents

Part 1

Part 2

Your Legal Companion

One of the most important and difficult choices you make when starting a business (whether by yourself or with others) is trying to figure out whether a limited liability company (LLC) or corporation will best meet your needs. An equally difficult decision occurs if you have already organized your business but want to explore the possibility of converting to a business entity with more favorable legal and tax characteristics.

In both cases, this book will help you with your decision.

Although the focus of this book is on choosing whether to form an LLC or corporation, you cannot make an informed decision without learning about all the types of business entities—including sole proprietorships, partnerships, LLCs, and corporations. This book explains the legal and tax characteristics of each of these business entities and the basic rules for converting one type of business to another.

This book also provides information about some of the less well-known ways of structuring a business. For example, two legal spin-offs of the basic partnership form—the limited partnership and the registered limited liability partnership—are discussed. This book also covers S corporations, which have some characteristics of the more well-known C corporation (including limited liability) but are taxed like a partnership.

I've divided this book into two parts.

Part One discusses basic information about each type of business entity. It includes the following chapters:

- Chapter 1 discusses each type of business entity, including the relative advantages and disadvantages of each.

- Chapter 2 explains how your choice of entities affects your personal liability for debts against your business.
- Chapter 3 examines the relative ease with which each of the entities can be formed and managed.
- Chapter 4 covers how each entity deals with profits, losses, investments, and taxes.
- Chapter 5 explains how doing business out of state may affect your choice of entity.

Part Two includes the following chapters:

- Chapter 6 discusses converting a sole proprietorship to another entity.
- Chapter 7 discusses converting a partnership to another entity.
- Chapter 8 discusses converting a limited liability company to another entity.
- Chapter 9 discusses converting a corporation to another entity, and reorganizing or dissolving a corporation.
- Chapter 10 provides examples of various conversion scenarios discussed in previous chapters.

This book also includes links you can use to find information regarding your state's corporate and LLC rules, as well as tax and securities laws information (see the appendix).

Business law and tax rules can get a bit complicated. Don't worry. They're presented here in real-life contexts, without off-putting legal or tax jargon, and without the technicalities best left to legal and tax professionals. By the time you finish this book, you'll understand what each type of entity has to offer, and you'll be ready to choose the right structure for your company. By the way, Nolo (www.nolo.com), the publisher of this book, provides many ways to assist you when it comes to corporations and LLCs, including assistance with state filings, helpful books, and lots of free information. Visit the site and click "Business, LLCs & Corporations," on the left side of the home page. ●

PART

1

Business Entity Basics

Now that you know why this is an important decision, it's time to learn some basic information about each type of business entity.

Sole Proprietorships

The simplest way to be in business for yourself is as a "sole proprietor." This is just a fancy way of saying that you are the owner of a one-person business. There's almost no cost or bureaucratic red tape involved in forming a sole proprietorship, other than the usual license, permit, and other regulatory requirements that your state and/or locality imposes on any business. And you don't have to do anything to create a sole proprietorship: If you start a one-person business and don't form a corporation or LLC, you have created a sole proprietorship, and that's how the state and the IRS will treat your business.

As a practical matter, most one-person businesses start out as sole proprietorships just to keep things simple.

> **EXAMPLE:** Winston is a graphic artist who started a sideline computer graphics business in his garage. Winston works only part time in his own business and has no employees. He has just a couple of clients and no pressing personal liability issues, so he chooses to operate as a sole proprietor (his other choices would be to form an LLC or a corporation). Outside of a business license, fictitious name filing, and tax permit, Winston does not need to file any legal paperwork. Unless Winston takes steps to change the legal structure of his business—by filing the necessary papers with his state to form a one-person LLC or corporation—his business will automatically be classified and treated as a sole proprietorship.

Number of Owners

By definition, a sole proprietorship has only one owner. If your one-person business grows and you wish to include other owners, you will

Businesses Owned by Spouses

Generally, if a husband and wife carry on an unincorporated business together and share in its profits and losses, they are considered the co-owners of a partnership, not a sole proprietorship, and they must file a partnership tax return for the business. However, there are a few exceptions to this rule.

One exception provides that if one spouse manages the business and the other helps out as an employee or volunteer worker (but does not contribute to running the business), the managing spouse can claim ownership and treat the business as a sole proprietorship.

Another exception is that the spouses can elect to divide up the profits of the business and report them separately for each spouse on their joint 1040 tax return, provided that:

- The business in unincorporated and is not a state-created business entity, such as an LLC or limited partnership.
- The only members of the business are a husband and wife who file a joint 1040 tax return.
- Both spouses materially participate in the trade or business.
- Both spouses elect not to be treated as a partnership (the spouses do not file a separate partnership return for the business).

They accomplish this reporting by filing a Schedule C for each spouse with their joint 1040 tax return, showing each spouse's share of profits on each Schedule C. Each spouse also includes a self-employment tax schedule (Schedule SE) to pay self-employment tax on each owner's share of the profits. If the spouses qualify for this exception, each spouse gets Social Security credit for his or her share of earnings in the business.

Finally, there is another special exception to partnership tax treatment available in several states. Specifically, IRS rules say that an unincorporated business (including an LLC) that is owned solely by a husband and wife as community property (and in community property states including Arizona, California, Idaho, Louisiana, Nevada, New Mexico, Texas, Washington, and Wisconsin), can treat itself as a sole

Businesses Owned by Spouses (cont'd)

proprietorship by filing an IRS Form 1040 Schedule C for the business, listing one of the spouses as the owner. Only the listed spouse pays income and self-employment taxes on the reported Schedule C net profits. This means only the listed Schedule C owner-spouse will receive Social Security account earning credits for the Form SE taxes paid with the 1040 return. For this reason, some eligible spouses will decide not to make this Schedule C filing and will continue to file partnership tax returns for their jointly-owned spousal LLC.

Also note that the IRS treats the filing of a Schedule C for a jointly owned spousal LLC as the conversion of a partnership to a sole proprietorship, which can also have tax consequences.

For more information on spousal businesses, see the section titled "Election for Husband and Wife Unincorporated Business," IRS Publication 541, in the section on "Forming a Partnership," and other information on the IRS website (www.irs.gov). In all cases, be sure to check with your tax adviser before deciding on the best way to own, file, and pay taxes for a spousal business.

need to choose another business structure, such as a partnership, LLC, or corporation.

Liability for Business Debts

Unfortunately, although forming and running a sole proprietorship is simple, it can also be risky. That's because sole proprietors are 100% personally liable for all business debts and legal claims. For example, if someone slips and falls in a sole proprietor's business and then sues, the owner is responsible for paying any resulting court award (unless commercial liability insurance covers it). Similarly, if the business fails to pay suppliers, banks, or bills from other businesses, the owner is personally liable for the unpaid debts. This means that the owner's personal assets, such as his or her bank accounts, equity in a house or car, and other personal assets can be taken by court order and sold to repay business debts and judgments.

Of course, some businesses are much more vulnerable to debts and lawsuits than others. If you run a part-time business that does not operate on credit and is unlikely to engender lawsuits, you probably don't need to worry about these issues. (Chapter 2 provides more information about personal liability.)

Income Taxation

Sole proprietors report their business profits or losses on IRS Schedule C, *Profit or Loss From Business (Sole Proprietorship)*, which they file with their 1040 individual federal tax returns. The owner's profits are taxed at his or her individual income tax rate. This is called "pass-through" taxation because the income passes through the business to the owner's individual tax return. In other words, like a partnership, a sole proprietorship is not taxed separately under the federal tax scheme.

Most start-up business owners prefer pass-through taxation of their business income, at least in the beginning. Why? Reporting and paying individual income taxes by preparing a Schedule C (and a Schedule SE for self-employment tax) are a lot easier than preparing a corporate tax return or dealing with partnership income taxes.

Because sole proprietors are self-employed, they have no employer to chip in part of their Social Security and Medicare taxes (called "self-employment taxes" for those working for themselves and "FICA taxes" for regular employees). Regular employees generally pay half of these taxes through payroll deductions, and the employer pays the other half. Sole proprietors must pay the entire amount themselves (by preparing Schedule SE, the *Self-Employment Tax* return, which must be filed along with a Schedule C and 1040 income tax return each year).

EXAMPLE: Two Web designers set up a side business to design websites for nonprofit organizations. They are too busy working to bother thinking about the best business structure for their new sideline business. Without taking any formal action or creating a partnership agreement, they have formed a partnership. If the partners were to have a dispute—over the division of profits, perhaps—in the absence of an agreement, state partnership law would control the outcome. Once they realize that their informality might subject them to rules that are not of their choosing, they decide to prepare a written partnership agreement.

Number of Partners

General partnerships may be formed by two or more people; by definition, there is no such thing as a one-person partnership. Legally, there is no upper limit on the number of partners who may be admitted into a partnership, but general partnerships with many owners tend to have problems reaching a consensus on business decisions and may be subject to divisive disputes among contending management factions. In larger partnerships, one or more partners may be designated as managing partners to eliminate day-to-day bickering, but delegating authority to a select group of managing partners is rare in small business partnerships. Why? Because doing so can be risky for the nonmanaging partners—who, by definition, won't be keeping a close eye on the business, but will still be personally liable for partnership debts. So, to minimize risks and keep all the partners honest, all general partners usually take an active hand in management.

Personal Liability for Business Debts

Each partner is personally liable for all business debts and any claims (including court judgments) against the partnership that the business can't pay. For example, if the business fails to pay its suppliers, the partners are personally responsible for paying these business debts and may have to mortgage their houses, sell their cars, and empty personal bank accounts to come up with the necessary cash.

And creditors don't have to respect the partners' internal arrangements about who owns what percentage of the company's assets or who is responsible for what share of the partnership's debts. If the business owes money it can't pay, the creditor may go after any general partner for the entire debt, regardless of his or her partnership ownership percentage. (If this happens, the partner who is sued can in turn sue the other partners to force them to repay their shares of the debt, but this can be costly and time-consuming.)

Personal liability for business debts is even more worrisome, because each general partner may bind the entire partnership (and all of the partners) to a contract or business deal. In legal jargon, each partner is an agent of the partnership, with the right to undertake obligations on its behalf. (Fortunately, there are a few significant limitations to this agency rule—to be valid, a contract or deal must generally be within the scope of the partnership's business, and the outside person who makes the deal with a partner must reasonably think that the partner is authorized to act on behalf of the partnership.)

If a partnership can't fulfill a valid contract or other business deal, each partner may be held personally liable for the amount owed. This personal liability for the debts of the entire partnership, coupled with the agency authority of each partner to bind the others, makes the general partnership riskier than a sole proprietorship (where only the proprietor can legally bind the business) and far riskier than entities such as LLCs, corporations, and limited partnerships, which offer at least some of the owners limited personal liability for business debts.

General Partnership Income Taxation

Like a sole proprietorship, a general partnership is treated as a pass-through tax entity. The profits (and losses) pass through the business entity to the partners, who pay taxes on any profits on their individual returns at their individual tax rates.

Partnership taxation is more complicated than sole proprietorship taxation, however, and most partnerships of any size will likely need a tax adviser who understands partnership tax and procedures. Although a partnership does not pay its own taxes, it must file an informational return each year, IRS Form 1065, *U.S. Return of Partnership Income.* In addition, the partnership must give each partner a filled-in IRS Schedule K-1 (Form 1065), *Partner's Share of Income, Deductions, Credits, etc.,* which shows the proportionate share of partnership profits or losses each person carries over to his or her individual 1040 tax return at the end of the year.

Each partner must pay taxes on his or her entire share of profits, even if the partnership chooses to reinvest the profits in the business rather than distributing all of them to the partners. The technical way of saying this is that the partners are taxed on their "allocated" profits, not on their "distributed" profits.

What about self-employment (Social Security and Medicare) taxes? Although general partners are not considered employees of the partnership, they must pay self-employment taxes on their share of partnership income.

> **TIP**
>
> **Self-employment tax rules may change.** Partners, LLC members, and S corporation shareholders can be treated differently when it comes to self-employment taxes, even though they are all owners of pass-through businesses. To deal with this inconsistency, the U.S. Treasury Department has been trying to revamp the entire self-employment tax scheme to make it apply uniformly to all of these entities. So far, final regulations have not been adopted, but everyone in the tax field expects an eventual change in how the self-employment tax rules apply to all multiowner pass-through tax entities: partnerships, LLCs, and S corporations alike. Ask your tax adviser for the latest information.

Limited Liability Companies (LLCs)

The limited liability company (LLC) is the newest kid on the block of business organizations. It has become popular with many small business owners, in part because it was custom-designed by state legislatures to overcome limitations of each of the other business forms—including the corporation. Essentially, the LLC is a business ownership structure that allows owners to pay business taxes on their individual income tax returns like partners (or, for a one-person LLC, like a sole proprietorship), but that also gives the owners the legal protection of personal limited liability for business debts and judgments as if they had formed a corporation. So, an LLC provides both pass-through taxation of business profits (like a partnership or sole proprietorship) and limited personal liability for business debts (like a corporation).

> **EXAMPLE:** Barry and Sam jointly own and run a flower shop, Aunt Jessica's Florals, which specializes in unique flower arrangements. Lately, business has been particularly rosy, and the two men plan to sign a long-term contract with a flower importer to supply them with larger quantities of seasonal flowers. Once they receive the additional flowers, they will be able to create more floral pieces and wholesale them to a wider market. Both men are sensitive to the fact that they will encounter more risks as their business grows. They decide to protect their personal assets from business risks by converting to an LLC. They could accomplish the same result by incorporating, but they prefer the simplicity of paying taxes on their business income on their individual income tax returns, rather than splitting business income between themselves and their corporation. If they begin making more money than each needs to take home, they can convert their LLC to a corporation to obtain lower corporate income tax rates on earnings kept in the business or, as an alternative, they can make an IRS election to have their LLC taxed as a corporation without changing its legal structure at all.

Number of Owners

In every state, you can form an LLC with only one member. LLC members need not be residents of the state where they form their LLC (or even the United States, for that matter), and other business entities, such as a corporation or another LLC, can be LLC owners.

Limited Liability

Under each state's LLC laws, the owners of an LLC are not personally liable for its debts and other liabilities. This personal legal liability protection is the same as that offered to shareholders of a corporation.

Pass-Through Taxation

Federal and state tax laws treat an LLC as a partnership—or, for a one-owner LLC, as a sole proprietorship. The LLC owners report LLC income, losses, credits, and deductions on their individual income tax returns. The LLC itself does not pay income tax. However, as with partnerships, there are "check-the-box" tax rules that allow an LLC to elect corporate tax treatment if its owners wish to leave income in the business and have it taxed at separate corporate income tax rates. Chapter 4 explains how corporate tax treatment works.

RESOURCE

Finding your state's LLC tax rules. Some states impose an annual fee or tax on LLCs, in addition to the individual income tax that owners pay on LLC profits allocated to them each year. To find out whether your state imposes an LLC tax, go to your state's tax department website. The appendix contains a link you can use to find state tax office website information.

Because a co-owned LLC is taxed as a partnership, it files standard partnership tax returns (IRS Form 1065 and Schedules K) with the IRS and the state, and the LLC owners pay taxes on their share of LLC profits on their individual income tax returns. (Each owner gets a Schedule K-1 from the LLC, which shows the owner's share of LLC profits and deductions. The owner attaches the K-1 to his or her individual income tax return.)

An LLC with only one owner is treated as a sole proprietorship for tax purposes. The owner includes profits or losses from the LLC's operations, as well as deductions and credits allowable to the business, on a Schedule C filed with the owner's individual income tax return.

If a sole-owner or multiowner LLC elects corporate tax treatment, the LLC is treated and taxed as a corporation, not as a sole proprietorship or partnership. The LLC files corporate income tax returns, reporting and paying corporate income tax on any profits retained in the LLC. The LLC members report and pay individual income tax only on salaries paid to them or distributions of LLC profits or losses that are paid as "dividends." However, as is true for partnerships, LLCs that may benefit from electing corporate tax treatment often decide to go ahead and incorporate. By doing so, they get corporate tax treatment plus the other "built-in" advantages the corporation provides, such as access to capital, capital sharing with employees, tax-deductible employee fringe benefits, and built-in management formalities.

Management

Most LLCs are managed by all the owners (also called members). This is known as "member-management." But state law also allows for management by one or more specially appointed managers, who may be members or nonmembers. Not surprisingly (but somewhat awkwardly), this arrangement is known as "manager-management." In other words, an LLC can appoint one or more of its members, or one of its CEOs, or even a person contracted from outside the LLC, to manage its affairs.

This manager setup is somewhat atypical for small, closely held LLCs; it makes sense only if one person wishes to assume full-time control of the LLC, while the other owners act as passive investors in the enterprise.

Formation Requirements

Like for a corporation, it takes some paperwork to get an LLC going. You must file a legal document (usually called articles of organization) with the state business filing office. And if the LLC will maintain a business presence in another state, such as a branch office, you must also file registration or qualification papers with the other state's business filing office. (For more on out-of-state requirements, see Chapter 5.) LLC formation fees vary, but most are comparable to the fee each state charges for incorporation.

Like a partnership, an LLC should prepare an operating agreement to spell out how the LLC will be owned, how profits and losses will be divided, how departing or deceased members will be bought out, and other essential ownership details. If you don't prepare an operating agreement, the default provisions of the state's LLC Act will apply to the operation of your LLC. Because virtually all LLC owners will want to control exactly how profits and losses are apportioned among the members (as well as other essential LLC operating rules), you'll want to prepare an LLC operating agreement.

RESOURCE

Want more information about LLCs? See *Form Your Own Limited Liability Company*, by Anthony Mancuso (Nolo), for instructions on how to form an LLC in each state, how to prepare an operating agreement, and how to handle other LLC formation requirements. You can also learn more about LLC formation procedures and fees for your state by visiting your state's business filing office website. You can find your state's business filing office website using the links in the appendix. Nolo (www.nolo.com), the publisher of this book, provides many ways to assist you when it comes to forming and creating an LLC. (The company can even assist you with filing.) Visit the Nolo site and click "Business, LLCs & Corporations," on the left side of the home page.

Corporations

A corporation, like an LLC, is a statutory creature, created and regulated by state law. In short, if you want the "privilege"—that's what the courts call it—of turning your business enterprise into a corporation, you must follow the requirements of your state's business corporation law or business corporation act (BCA). What sets the corporation apart, in a theoretical sense, from all other types of businesses is that it is a legal and tax entity separate from any of the people who own, control, manage, or operate it.

Federal and state laws view the corporation as a legal "person," which means that the corporation can enter into its own contracts, incur its own debts, and pay its own taxes, separate and apart from its owners.

For tax purposes, there are two types of corporations: C corporations and S corporations. A C corporation is just another name for a regular for-profit corporation—a corporation taxed under normal corporate income tax rules. The letter C comes from Subchapter C of the Internal Revenue Code and is used to distinguish these regular corporations from S corporations, a more specialized type of corporation that is regulated under Subchapter S of the Internal Revenue Code.

An S corporation gets the pass-through tax treatment of a partnership (with some important technical differences) and the limited liability of a corporation, much like an LLC. This section covers the more common and widely accepted C corporation. (S corporations are discussed in more detail below.)

To form a corporation, you pay corporate filing fees and prepare and file formal organizational papers, usually called "articles of incorporation," with a state agency (in most states, the secretary or department of state). Once formed, the corporation assumes an independent legal life separate from its owners. This separate legal life leads to a number of familiar traditional corporate characteristics, discussed below.

Number of Shareholders (Owners) and Directors

A corporation can have as many or as few shareholders as it wants. However, every corporation needs directors and officers to manage and run its day-to-day business. In most states, it is possible to set up a one-person corporation, in which one person acts as the sole shareholder, director, president, secretary, and treasurer of the corporation.

Limited Liability for Shareholders

A corporation provides all of its owners—that is, its shareholders—with the benefits of limited personal liability protection. If a court judgment is entered against the corporation or the corporation can't pay its bills, only the corporation's assets are at stake. The shareholders stand to lose only the money that they've invested; creditors cannot go after their personal assets.

Traditionally, business owners formed corporations primarily to wrap themselves in the legal mantle of limited liability to avoid personal exposure to business debts and claims. Of course, now that LLCs have entered the picture, small business owners can choose between the two entity types if they are looking for limited liability protection.

C Corporation Income Taxation

In an unincorporated business, the owners pay individual income taxes on all net profits of the business, regardless of how much they actually receive each year. For example, assume that a partnership or an LLC has two owners and earns $100,000 in net profits. If the owners split profits equally, each must report and pay individual income taxes on $50,000 of business profits. This is true even if all of the profits are kept in the business checking account to meet upcoming business expenses—not paid out to the owners.

In contrast, a corporation is a legal entity separate from its shareholders and files its own tax return, paying taxes on any profits left in the business. Unlike LLC members, shareholders who work for the corporation are treated as employees who receive salaries for their work in the business. The corporation deducts owners' salaries as a business expense when it computes its net taxable income. But because the owners of a small corporation also manage the business as its directors, they have the luxury (within reasonable limits) of deciding how much to pay themselves in salary. In short, the owners decide how much of the profits will be taxed at the corporate level and how much will be paid out to them and taxed on their individual returns.

Two results follow from this:

- The owners pay individual income taxes on salary amounts they actually receive, not on all the net profits of the business.
- The corporation—which, remember, is a separate tax entity—pays corporate taxes on the net profits retained in the business.

In effect, the corporate tax scheme is more accurate, because it taxes the business only for profits actually retained in the business, while taxing the owners only on profits they actually receive. This type of income-splitting between the company and the owners can lead to tax savings.

The corporation's owners file individual income tax returns and pay taxes, at their individual tax rates, on the salaries and any bonuses they receive. At the end of the year, the corporation files a corporate tax return, IRS Form 1120, *U.S. Corporation Income Tax Return,* and pays its own income taxes on the profits left in the company. Corporate tax rates (see "Tax Rates on Taxable Corporate Income," below) are lower than most shareholders' individual tax rates for the first $75,000 of income (profits are taxed at 15% for the first $50,000, and 25% for the next $25,000). So, if the owners decide to retain profits in the business for expansion or other business needs, nontaxable income of up to $75,000 will be taxed at rates that typically are lower than the owners' individual tax rates, resulting in an overall tax savings.

Tax Rates on Taxable Corporate Income	
$0 to $50,000	15%
$50,001 to $75,000	25%
$75,001 to $100,000	34%
$100,001 to $335,000	39%
$335,001 to $10,000,000	34%
$10,000,001 to $15,000,000	35%
$15,000,001 to $18,333,333	38%
Over $18,333,333	35%
Note: Personal service corporations are subject to a flat tax of 35% regardless of how much they earn.	

EXAMPLE: Justine and Janine are partners in Just Jams & Jellies, a specialty store selling gourmet canned preserves. Business has boomed, and the owners' net taxable income has reached a level where it is taxed at an individual tax rate of 35%. If the owners incorporate, they can leave $75,000 worth of nontaxable income in their business, which will be taxed at the lower corporate tax rates of 15% and 25%. This saves Justine and Janine significant dollars when tax time rolls around.

Some small businesses, however, don't need this corporate tax strategy (known as "income-splitting"); instead of leaving some money in the business, their owners wish to pay out all net profits to themselves at the end of each tax year.

EXAMPLE 1: Winston set up his own computer graphics company as a sideline to his day job. Like many other small service business owners, he does not reinvest the profits of his self-employment business, but happily deposits every last cent into his own personal checking account. Corporate tax treatment will not benefit Winston, because he doesn't accumulate money in his business.

EXAMPLE 2: Linux and Colleen own and work part time for their own LLC, a retail sales business that employs one full-time worker, Vince. Linux and Colleen share in the LLC's profits as owners, not employees (the normal set-up for LLC members). Gross sales revenue of the business this year is expected to be $200,000. Cost of inventory sold will be $50,000, so net sales revenue is $150,000. Linux and Colleen annually pay Vince $50,000 in salary and their landlord $25,000 to rent their storefront property. Other normal business expenses total about $20,000 per year, so the net profits will be about $55,000. The owners need to pay out all of this money to themselves for their hard work and to help meet their own living expenses (they also rely on their personal savings to help them get by as their business gets going). Again, as in the example above, income-splitting is not a viable tax strategy here, because the owners need to take all of the profits out of the business.

But for other small businesses, even those with modest net incomes, the corporate tax strategy may be worthwhile. Many small business owners have to retain profits in their businesses to handle upcoming costs of doing business, purchase inventory, pay employee salaries, and fund their other necessary and regular business expenses, such as rent and insurance. Owners might need to retain net profits in the business even if they are not paying themselves as much in profits as they would like. In these situations, being able to pay the lower corporate tax rates on net income left in the business may result in tax savings.

> **EXAMPLE:** Let's imagine Linux and Colleen a few years from now. Their LLC is making more money. For the past two years, their gross sales have averaged $500,000, and their cost of inventory sold has remained level at 25% of gross sales, or $125,000. Vince, the only full-time employee, and the owners have had to work harder to meet increased customer demand, giving up many of their weekends to the business. Vince's salary has increased to $75,000, but other expenses have stayed almost level at $60,000. Net LLC profits now average $240,000 per year, with each owner taking home a $120,000 share.
>
> Linux and Colleen agree to look for a slightly more upscale storefront, hoping to sell more-expensive items (with higher margins) to a more-affluent clientele. They know that they'll have to come up with a lot of money to move into a new space, and they also expect to need additional funds to start stocking the higher-priced inventory. In addition, they discuss the possibility of hiring another full-time worker—if only to allow themselves to have more weekend time away from the business. They each realize they'll have to take a temporary cut in their share of paid-out profits to fund the move and expansion. Realizing they will need to begin retaining a substantial amount of LLC profits in the business in order to accomplish these plans, they decide to elect corporate tax treatment so that the profits kept in the business will be taxed at lower corporate income tax rates.

Now for one last income tax item: When a corporation is sold or dissolved, the shareholders and their corporation must each pay taxes on any increased value (appreciation) of assets owned by the corporation. This means that a double tax is paid on the same appreciation—once by the corporation and again by its owners. For businesses that own real estate or buy other types of property that are likely to increase in value, this can be a big disadvantage. The rules here are complex and tricky—

just realize that one of the more technical issues of deciding whether to incorporate has to do with the tax consequences that will occur when you sell or dissolve your business. This is definitely one area where you'll want some expert tax advice before making your decision.

Corporate Management

Because a corporation has a legal existence separate from its owners, you must pay more attention to its legal care and feeding than you would for a sole proprietorship, a partnership, or an LLC.

Corporations are owned by shareholders and managed by a board of directors. This means that the owners of a small corporation must periodically wear different legal hats. As directors, they must hold annual meetings required by state law. They must also keep minutes of meetings, prepare formal documentation (in the form of resolutions or written consents to corporate actions) of important decisions made during the life of the corporation, and keep a paper trail of all legal and financial dealings between the corporation and its shareholders.

Making corporate life even more complicated, the board of directors must appoint officers to supervise daily corporate business. State law usually requires the board to appoint at least a president (CEO), a secretary, and a treasurer. In practice, however, because a small corporation's shareholders usually act as both its board of directors and its officers, this simply means that one person or a few people are going to hold several corporate titles.

> **EXAMPLE:** Tornado Air Conditioning Service, Inc., is owned and operated by Ted and his spouse, Valerie. They name themselves as the only two directors in the corporate articles they file with the state. At the first organizational meeting of the board, they appoint Valerie as both President and Treasurer, and Ted as both corporate VP and Secretary. They also approve the issuance of the corporation's initial shares to Ted and Valerie, its only two shareholders.

Corporate Capital and Stock Structure

A corporation issues stock to its shareholders in exchange for capital they invest in the business. The way in which corporate stock allows corporations to structure ownership remains unique in the world of business entities and leads to a few special benefits. For example, a corporation can parcel out ownership interests in the form of shares, which can be divided into classes, each with different rights to vote, receive dividends, and receive cash if the business is liquidated.

Corporate stock is also a very useful way to fund employee stock option or bonus plans. In addition, you can use it to fund a buyout of another business or exchange or convert it into the shares of another corporation to effect a merger or consolidation. And, of course, the corporate stock structure is almost essential if a business wants to raise money from the public in an initial public offering (IPO). The state corporation statutes flesh out the full potential of corporate stock ownership and provide legal rules procedures that are used throughout the banking, investment, and legal community to funnel private and public capital into corporate coffers.

Employee Fringe Benefits

Even small corporations have the opportunity to offer fringe benefits—such as group term-life and medical reimbursement plans—to their employees, as well as stock purchase, option, and incentive plans. The owner/employees who receive these benefits normally do not have to pay tax on the value of these benefits. And the corporation can generally deduct the cost of providing these benefits.

... And the Runners-Up: Limited Partnerships, S Corporations, and RLLPs

The preceding sections discuss the four most common business entities: sole proprietorships, partnerships, limited liability companies, and corporations. This section covers a few less common variations on some of these entities. Although these entities may not be well-known, they offer advantages for certain kinds of businesses—so you should consider them before making your final decision about what type of business to form.

Limited Partnerships

A limited partnership is similar to a general partnership, except it has two types of partners. A limited partnership must have at least one general partner, who manages the business and is personally liable for its debts and claims. (General partners have the same broad rights and responsibilities as the partners discussed in the general partnership section, above.) And, by definition, a limited partnership must also have at least one limited partner, and usually has more. A limited partner is typically an investor who contributes capital to the business but is not involved in day-to-day management. The limited partners are not personally liable for business debts and claims. They function much like passive shareholders in a small corporation, investing with the expectation of receiving a share of both profits and the eventual increase in the value of the business.

Liability

A limited partnership must have at least one general partner who is personally liable for the debts and other liabilities of the business (unless the general partner goes to the trouble of setting up his or her own corporation or LLC, which is discussed below). This differs from the structure of corporations and LLCs, in which all members are automatically covered by the cloak of limited liability protection.

As long as limited partners do not participate in management, they do not have personal liability for business debts and claims. However, if limited partners participate in decision making, this shield disappears, and they will be subject to personal liability for business debts. For that reason, if an owner of a limited partnership wants the benefit of limited liability protection, he or she must step back from active management of the business and invest in it as a passive investor only—something that is all but impossible for the millions of small business owners who plan to be active in their own businesses.

Income Taxation

For income tax purposes, limited partnerships generally are treated like general partnerships, with all partners individually reporting and paying taxes on their share of the profits each year. The limited partnership files an informational partnership tax return (IRS Form 1065, *U.S. Return of Partnership Income*, the same tax form that applies to a general partnership), and each partner receives IRS Schedule K-1 (1065), *Partner's Share of Income, Deductions, Credits, etc.*, from the partnership. Each partner then files this form with his or her individual IRS 1040 tax return. Limited partners, as a rule, do not have to pay self-employment taxes—because they are not active in the business, their share of partnership income is not considered "earned income" for purposes of the self-employment tax.

Management

As noted, limited partners are generally prohibited from managing the business. Some states have carved out some new exceptions to this ban, however, usually to allow a limited partner to vote on issues that affect the basic structure of the partnership, including the removal of general partners, terminating the partnership, amending the partnership agreement, or selling all or most of the assets of the partnership. If all owners want to be active in their company, they are probably better off forming an LLC or a corporation, which would allow all owners/investors to run the business while enjoying the protection of limited liability for business debts.

Although this business form is less versatile than an LLC, some companies still operate as limited partnerships. This usually happens in investment firms, where the investors insist that the managers of the company (the general partners) be on the hook for bad business decisions—the investors believe that the managers will be less likely to make unsound investments if their personal assets are at stake. But in other, usually larger, limited partnerships, the general partner is actually a limited liability enterprise such as an LLC or a corporation. This allows the general partner to avoid personal liability altogether.

EXAMPLE: In 1985, Situs Holdings, a limited partnership, was established as a real estate development company. Its general partner is The Situs Corporation, and it has 20 limited partners. The limited partners are individuals who invest money to purchase and improve the company's real estate holdings, while the general partner, The Situs Corporation, manages Situs Holdings' properties in exchange for a management fee. The Situs Corporation is owned by Sid Block and his two daughters, Elizabeth and Jackie. All of the partners (The Situs Corporation and the limited partners) share in a percentage of the profits of Situs Holdings.

Note that the general partner is a corporation. This is a standard technique used to limit the personal liability of the general partner in larger limited partnerships, particularly if the liabilities of the company may be hefty. In this situation, the company's real estate debts are substantial, and the potential liabilities associated with the renovation and sale of properties are also considerable—general contractor liability claims, purchaser rescissions, and other disputes that may end up in court can go into the million-dollar range. Of course, the whole Situs ownership scheme was established before the LLC came into existence. If Sid and his daughters and the limited partners had to do it all over again, their legal and tax advisers would probably recommend a much simpler setup—namely, forming one manager-managed LLC to hold and develop the properties. All of the LLC managers and the nonmanaging members (the investors) would enjoy limited liability protection.

Forming a Limited Partnership

To create a limited partnership, you must pay an initial fee and file papers with the state—usually a "certificate of limited partnership." This document is similar to the articles (or certificate) filed by a corporation or an LLC and includes information about the general and limited partners. Filing fees are about the same for limited partnerships as for a corporation or an LLC.

S Corporations

An S corporation is a corporation that qualifies for special tax treatment under the Internal Revenue Code (and state corporate tax statutes as well). To form one, you'll have to jump through the same state incorporation hoops as you would to form a regular C corporation. This means you have to file articles of incorporation with the state and pay a state filing fee. Then, to elect S corporation tax treatment, the shareholders must sign and file an S corporation tax election, IRS Form 2253 (and possibly a separate S tax election with the state tax agency). But as you'll see below, choosing S corporation status is a tax, not a legal, election—the same legal corporation rules applicable to C corporations also apply to S corporations.

> ⊙ **TIP**
>
> **LLCs have largely replaced S corporations.** Formerly, the only way that all owners of a business could obtain personal liability protection while retaining pass-through taxation of business income was to form an S corporation. Since the arrival of the LLC, however, S corporations have largely fallen out of favor. The LLC provides substantially the same benefits as an S corporation without several of the significant restrictions of S corporations (discussed below).

Number of Shareholders (Owners) and Directors

Generally, an S corporation may have no more than 100 shareholders (a husband and wife and certain other family members count as one shareholder), all of whom must be either individuals who are U.S. citizens or residents, or certain types of trusts or estates. While the 100-shareholder limit may not be much of an inconvenience—after all, most small businesses have fewer than five owners—the other shareholder restrictions can be significant.

Limited Liability for Shareholders

Because S corporations are the same legally as C corporations under state law, all S corporation shareholders have limited personal liability protection from the debts and other liabilities of the corporation.

S Corporation Income Taxation

Once a corporation makes an S corporation tax election, its profits and losses pass through the corporation and are reported on the individual tax returns of the S corporation's shareholders. This means that any profits an S corporation retains at the end of the year are not taxed at the business entity level at corporate tax rates (as is the case for a regular C corporation), but instead are allocated through to the S corporation's owners.

In other words, S corporation profits are allocated and taxed to each shareholder each year at the shareholder's individual income tax rates (this is the same basic pass-through tax treatment afforded partnership and LLC owners).

S Corporations Compared to LLCs

Before the LLC business form came along, forming an S corporation was the preferred way for business owners to obtain personal liability protection while retaining pass-through taxation of business income. However, now that the LLC is on the scene, S corporations no longer hold much allure for most business owners. Here's why:

- **Formation requirements.** To form an S corporation, you must first form a regular C corporation, then elect S corporation tax treatment by filing an S corporation tax election with the IRS. This involves more paperwork than simply forming an LLC.

- **Corporate formalities.** S corporation shareholders, like LLC members, are protected from personal liability for the debts of the business. But to keep this limited liability protection, you have to follow corporate rules when running your business. This means that you have to issue stock, elect officers, hold regular board of directors' and shareholders' meetings, keep corporate minutes of all meetings, and follow the mandatory rules found in your state's corporation code. By contrast, if you form an LLC, you won't have to jump through most of these legal hoops—you just have to make sure your management team is in agreement on major decisions and go about your business. Although it makes sense to hold formal LLC meetings from time to time to record important management decisions, *you* get to decide when you really need to do this.

- **Ownership restrictions.** Because S corporation stock may be owned only by individuals who are U.S. citizens or residents, it doesn't have the same organizational flexibility of the LLC. (Special types of trusts and other special entities can own S corporation shares, too, but these exceptions don't help the average business person.) Even if an S corporation initially meets the U.S. citizen (or resident) requirement, its shareholders can't sell their shares to a foreign citizen or to a company (like a corporation or an LLC), on pain of losing S corporation tax status. (Also, S corporations can have only one class of stock. The result of these ownership restrictions is that some of the C corporation's main benefits—namely, the ability to set up employee stock option and bonus plans, and to bring in venture and public capital—are pretty much out of the question.) In contrast, any type of person or entity can become an LLC member: a U.S. citizen, a citizen of a foreign country, another LLC, a corporation, or a limited partnership. Finally, LLCs have the flexibility to set up different classes of ownership.

- **Required allocation of profits and losses.** S corporation's profits and losses must be distributed to the shareholders in proportion to their stockholdings. LLCs have more flexibility in this regard; they can tailor the allocations of profits and losses to meet the needs of investors—for example, an LLC can bring in an investor for a share of LLC profits or losses that is disproportionately larger than his or her capital interest.

EXAMPLE: Ely and Natalie want to go into business designing solar-powered hot tubs. Ely is the "money" person and agrees to pitch in 80% of the first-year funds necessary to get the business going. Natalie is the hot tub and solar specialist and will operate the business. One-half of Natalie's first-year salary, plus a cash payment of $20,000, will fund her initial 20% share in the enterprise. In exchange for Ely's investment, the two agree that Ely will receive two-thirds of the profits of the business for five years, at which point they will be divided equally. While doling out profits in a way that is disproportionate to business ownership makes practical sense for Ely and Natalie, it is not permitted under S corporation rules. Far better for Ely and Natalie to form an LLC, which does allow them this flexibility (as long as they comply with technical tax rules).

- **Limitations of S corporation tax treatment.** A full discussion of S corporation taxes is beyond the scope of this book. Nevertheless, one aspect of S corporations can make a huge difference to some business investors. Generally, the tax advantages associated with an S corporation's business debts cannot be passed along to its shareholders unless they have personally loaned the company the money. This means an S corporation shareholder's tax basis in the business normally does not increase when the company takes on debt. Conversely, LLCs can give their owners the tax benefits of most business debt, regardless of the source of the funds, which means that the owners' tax basis in the business will increase when the company takes on debt. Because distributions of profits from the LLC are taxable to the owner only when they exceed the owner's tax basis in the company, this increase in basis means that each of the LLC owners is less likely to be taxed on profits paid to them. So, if a company will incur substantial debt (as would often be the case if it borrows money to open its business or buy real estate), investors who form an S corporation will be at a disadvantage relative to an LLC.

EXAMPLE: An LLC borrows $400,000 from a bank. This debt is allocated equally to four LLC owners. This means it increases each owner's tax basis in his capital (ownership) interest. This basis increase, in turn, means that each owner can receive $100,000 in distributions of profits from the LLC tax-free (distributions are only taxed when they exceed an owner's basis). By contrast, S corporation shareholders do not receive an increased basis in their shares when the corporation borrows money from a bank, so a loan of this sort would not provide a tax benefit to them.

S corporation owners do enjoy one advantage over LLCs members: They don't have to pay self-employment taxes (Social Security and Medicare taxes) on their share of business profits. S corporation shareholders normally do not have to pay self-employment taxes on any portion of S corporation profits that pass through to them at the end of each year. (If a shareholder is also employed by the S corporation, the corporation and the shareholder pay half of these taxes on the amount of the employee's salary only—not on any additional distributions of profit the shareholder receives as an owner of the company.) As of this writing, the self-employment tax situation for LLC owners is not officially settled. Currently, the general understanding is that LLC members who are active in their business should pay self-employment taxes on profits that pass through to them at the end of the year, which means that they must pay more in self-employment taxes than if they had formed an S corporation. In other words, not only do LLC members have to pay self-employment taxes on any salary (or other guaranteed payments) they receive, but they also must pay these taxes on all of the company's profits that are allocated to them.

> **EXAMPLE:** Sam owns a one-person S corporation that nets $250,000 in profits (before paying Sam's salary). Sam pays himself $100,000 as salary, and the remaining $150,000 is automatically allocated to him at the end of the year as his share of corporate profits. (Because an S corporation is a pass-through tax entity, all of the money is credited to Sam for tax purposes.) Sam pays income taxes and self-employment taxes only on the first $100,000; for the next $150,000, he pays only income taxes, not self-employment taxes. By contrast, if Sam had organized his business as a one-person LLC, his tax adviser probably would have advised him to pay self-employment taxes on the entire amount.

Disadvantages of the S Corporation Compared to the C Corporation

Because of the S corporation's ownership restrictions and its inability to issue special classes of stock, the S corporation is a lot less flexible than a regular C corporation when it comes to attracting key employees and investment capital. Because an S corporation cannot have more than 100 shareholders, it can't make a public offering of its shares, and because an S corporation can have only one class of shares, it can't easily accommodate the needs of outside venture capital firms and other investors who require special dividend or conversion rights in return for a capital investment in the company.

Registered Limited Liability Partnerships (RLLPs)

In all 50 states, professionals may set up a special type of partnership, called a registered limited liability partnership (RLLP), as an alternative to forming an LLC. In some states (like California), this new type of ownership structure was invented because state law didn't allow many professionals to form LLCs. In others, this business structure was established to help professionals in a multimember practice avoid personal liability for the malpractice of the other professionals in their firm. Unless you are forming a professional practice along with professional co-owners, the RLLP is probably not for you—check with a lawyer or tax adviser to be sure.

An RLLP is basically a partnership in which all of the owners remain personally liable for their own acts (malpractice) but receive limited liability for any malpractice of other partners in the firm. Most state RLLP statutes also give the professionals personal liability protection from other tort liabilities (personal injury lawsuits) of the RLLP as well as from business debts.

Number of Partners

You need at least two partners to form an RLLP. Typically, under state statutes, the partners must be licensed in the same or related professions. Professionals that are eligible to form an RLLP often include people who work in the legal, medical, and accounting fields, as well as in a short list of other professions in which a special "professional-client" relationship is assumed to exist. Some states also allow engineers, veterinarians, acupuncturists, and other professionals to form RLLPs. In some states, however, some types of licensed professionals are not allowed to form an RLLP.

TIP

Professionals eligible to form professional corporations can usually form RLLPS. The list of professionals who may form an RLLP in a particular state is often identical to the list of professionals eligible to form a professional corporation. For example, physicians can incorporate only as a professional corporation in most states, and are also eligible to form an RLLP in those states. Call your state LLC filing office to find out which professionals are eligible to form RLLPs in your state.

Limited Liability

RLLP owners enjoy a benefit not available to the owners of other partnerships: While the owners remain liable for the financial consequences of their own malpractice, they are not liable for the malpractice of the other professionals in their partnership. In addition, in more than half of the states, a partner in an RLLP is not personally liable for any type of liability, whether it arises from a contract, a tort, or the professional malpractice of another professional in the firm. This sort of sweeping protection is known as "full shield" limited liability protection.

RESOURCE

Look up your state's RLLP act. You can look up your state's RLLP act on the Internet through Nolo's Legal Research Center at www.nolo.com/legal-research. Click "State Law Resources," select the name of your state, and then either do a search or browse your state's code to find the RLLP act.

Before you form or convert to an RLLP, it's important to find out how much personal limited liability protection your state RLLP statute provides. In addition to reading your state's law yourself, one good way to do this is to consult your professional trade or licensing organization; they almost surely keep up with the law in this area. Because the wording of these state RLLP statutes varies widely, it's a good idea to consult with a knowledgeable business lawyer in your state to find out just how much protection your state RLLP statute provides.

RLLP Income Taxation

Like partnerships and LLCs, RLLPs are taxed as pass-through tax entities. This means that the owners are taxed on RLLP profits on their individual income tax returns at their individual tax rates; the RLLP itself is not taxed on profits under federal tax law and in most states. In most professional firms that provide services and not goods, this makes sense, because all profits are usually available to be paid out to the professionals each year—there is rarely any need to accumulate funds in professional service firms (as there often is in a nonservice business that needs to accumulate earnings for inventory, equipment, or future expansion).

RLLPs Compared to LLCs

For practical purposes, RLLPs are very similar to LLCs. They both have pass-through taxation and provide limited personal liability. The big difference is that RLLP professionals are protected from the malpractice of their partners, while LLC members are not. This is not a problem for the typical LLC owner—legal liability in most businesses comes about as a result of contract disputes, accidents on the premises (for example, slip-and-fall injuries), customer or product complaints, and the like—not as a result of an owner's direct, negligent conduct toward a client. But, of course, in a professional practice, things are very different; here, professionals are routinely sued for harm allegedly caused by the professional's own actions.

No matter how a professional sets up practice—as a partnership, LLC, RLLP, or professional corporation—the professional remains personally liable under state law for professional malpractice. Under RLLP statutes, however, professionals are often exempt from personal liability for the malpractice of other professionals whom they do not manage or control. This type of extra protection from "vicarious" professional malpractice is normally not provided under state LLC statutes.

One other difference between the LLC and the RLLP is in their ability to distribute profits freely. Many professional firms want the ability to distribute all net profits of the business to its owners. After all, most professional firms offer services rather than goods and do not need to keep profits in the company to accumulate inventory, buy expensive equipment, or expand the enterprise. But, technically, under most state LLC (and corporate) laws, LLCs cannot make distributions to owners if doing so would make the business insolvent—that is, unable to pay its debts as they become due—or would cause the business's liabilities to exceed its assets by a certain percent. An RLLP normally isn't subject to these limits. As a practical matter, however, many LLCs will not want to distribute every last penny of profits to owners each year, so these technical limitations won't matter to them.

Many states allow a professional to form either an LLC or an RLLP. Some states prohibit licensed professionals (such as doctors, lawyers, accountants, and engineers) from forming an LLC, and only permit them to form an RLLP (or, alternatively, a professional corporation). In California, certain licensed professionals such as doctors, lawyers, and accountants are prohibited from forming LLCs, and only lawyers, accountants, and architects can form RLLPs. So, if your practice is not one of these three professions, you have to form a professional corporation in California to limit your legal liability. Note that the rules regarding professionals are subject to change. Check with an attorney before deciding on the proper entity for your professional practice.

RLLPs Compared to Professional Corporations

The requirements for forming a professional corporation under state law are very similar to the requirements for forming an RLLP. For example, under typical state statutes, professional corporations, like RLLPs, must be owned by licensed professionals, must carry state-mandated amounts of professional malpractice insurance, and must adopt a name that meets the requirements of the state licensing board that regulates the profession.

In most states, an RLLP provides the same basic limited liability protection for professionals as a professional corporation. Modern RLLP statutes, however, typically contain explicit language that makes it clear that professionals are protected from tort, contract, and vicarious malpractice liability. State corporate statues sometimes are not so explicit. Before making the choice, review the full range of legal liability protection provided under your state's professional corporation statutes (versus its RLLP laws).

A major difference between RLLPs and professional corporations is their tax treatment. Professional corporations and their shareholders are subject to two levels of taxes—corporate- and individual-level income taxes—just like regular corporations, plus they have to contend with special corporate tax provisions. For example, the net profits of a "professional service corporation," a category defined to include many types of professional corporations formed under state law, are taxed at a flat 35% corporate tax, not at the graduated corporate tax rates that apply to the net profits of regular corporations. And professional service corporations also get lesser tax breaks, such as a smaller accumulated business income tax credit, which means they can become targets for additional tax penalties for retaining net profits in the corporation.

The Series LLC—A Rising Star on the Business Entity Horizon

A new type of LLC—known as the series LLC—is taking shape in a growing minority of states.

The main characteristic and advantage of the series LLC is that it allows the LLC to set up one or more series of assets within the LLC and each series of assets is administratively separate from the other series. That means that a series LLC can consist of separate businesses and properties all subsumed into the one LLC entity. However, the business and assets of each series can be managed and operated separately from the others. For example, each series can have separate owners and managers, separate operating agreements (specifying separate divisions of profits and losses associated with the series), and other separate formation and operation characteristics.

Under series LLC statutes in some states, each series of assets is insulated from the liabilities of the other series within the LLC. In these states, assets such as real estate can be put into separate series within an LLC, and each asset or property will be subject only to its own financing obligations (mortgages, equity lines of credit, and the like), not the financing obligations of assets or property placed within other series. This consolidation of assets in one LLC coupled with a separation of liability between the assets in each series can be of particular advantage to organizers who want to set up one LLC to develop, encumber, and sell multiple parcels of real estate.

Before you jump on the series LLC bandwagon, there are several cautions to keep in mind. For one, a state that does not have a series LLC statute may not respect the special characteristics of a series LLC formed in another state. And even if a state allows for the formation of a series LLC, its provisions may differ from the provisions of another state's series LLC law. This means that one state that permits a series LLC may not respect all the legal protections granted under the series LLC statutes of another state. Go to your state's business entity filing website (see the appendix) to see if your state allows the formation of a series LLC.

The Series LLC—A Rising Star on the Business Entity Horizon (cont'd)

There are other uncertainties. It's not yet clear whether a federal bankruptcy court will respect the separateness of each series within an LLC. For example, if one series in an LLC files for bankruptcy, it's not clear whether a bankruptcy court will reach out and attach the assets of the other series in the LLC in order to satisfy the bankrupt series' creditor claims.

Some entrepreneurs may form a series LLC to avoid paying formation and annual fees for multiple LLC entities. For example, if one series LLC is formed for six separate properties, the organizers will pay one filing fee—not six—when the series LLC is formed. Some states, however, may not be willing to forgo these filing fees so easily. For example, the California Franchise Tax Board, the state tax agency that assesses an $800 franchise tax payment plus an annual added gross receipts fee of up to $12,000 per year on each LLC formed or operating within the state, has stated that it will treat each series of an out-of-state LLC as a separate LLC.

This means that a Delaware series LLC that operates or owns property in California may have to pay the annual California franchise and any added tax for each series within the LLC. Similarly, when you register your series LLC in a state that does not have a series LLC statute, the state may decide that you owe a registration fee for each series in your LLC, not just one for the whole LLC.

It will take time for the states to develop their series LLC statutes and to coordinate and reconcile the laws, fees, and tax treatments among the states. Once this happens, and once the courts settle some of the legal nuances associated with this new form of business entity, the series LLC may indeed become the next big new thing in business entity formations.

Personal Liability Concerns

L imited liability is the issue that looms largest for many entrepreneurs when shopping around for the right business form. After
all, your business probably will be leveraged to some extent with
debt, such as revolving lines of credit from suppliers or a working capital
line of credit from a bank. If possible, you would probably like to avoid
being personally liable for the repayment of credit lines and business
loans you use to fill in the gaps in cash flow from one month to the next.
And, of course, you may be justifiably concerned about personal liability
for other legal claims against your business, such as:

- lawsuits over unpaid bills

- contract disputes

- slip-and-fall or other personal injuries that occur on business
  property

- damage your employees cause to others in the regular course of
  business, such as automobile accident damage, and

- local, state, and federal assessments of civil fines and penalties for
  regulatory violations.

If you start doing business without making a state filing—that is,
without forming a corporation, limited liability company, or other
liability-limiting entity—you have automatically formed a sole proprietorship (if your business has one owner) or a general partnership (if
your business has co-owners). The owners of sole proprietorships and
general partnerships are personally liable for business debts and claims.

This chapter takes a look at liability, discusses the use of liability-
limiting entities, and explains how insurance coverage can limit your
liability.

How Your Choice of Business Entity Affects Personal Liability

Liabilities are debts: money you owe. Every business carries some liabilities—for example, ongoing payments to suppliers, rent for your office, compensation to employees, or fees for contractors. Additional liabilities may arise if your business is devastated by a fire or flood or if you are the victim of a lawsuit—for example, someone is injured in your studio and sues you for damages. This section explains how the various types of business entities may or may not shield you from personal liability. Later in this chapter I discuss using insurance as a way to limit liability.

Sole Proprietorships and General Partnerships

Sole proprietorships and general partnerships offer no liability protection. If you operate your business as a sole proprietorship—the most common form for businesses—then you will be personally liable for all business debts. The same is true for a partnership. A creditor can collect a partnership debt from any partner, regardless of which partner incurred the debt. That means that if your partner orders $50,000 worth of equipment (without telling you) and then moves to Venezuela, you could be on the hook. A written partnership agreement can apportion liability among partners, but it won't absolve you of personal liability.

Limited Liability Entities

Corporations and limited liability companies (LLCs) (and certain other business forms, such as limited partnerships) shield their owners from personal liability. For a dramatic example of how this shield works to deflect liability, consider the recent demise of a 52-store chain. The company owed millions to suppliers and filed for bankruptcy, but the owners were not personally liable for these debts because they had created a corporate entity that owned the company.

If you operate as a corporation or LLC, creditors can—with some exceptions discussed below—collect their debts only from the business's assets, not from the owners. This means that a person who invests in an LLC, corporation, or limited partnership stands to lose only the amount of money or the value of the property that he or she has paid for an ownership interest. As a result, if the business does not succeed and cannot pay its debts or other financial obligations, creditors cannot seize or sell the owner's home, car, or other personal assets.

> **EXAMPLE:** Rackafrax Dry Cleaners, Inc., a corporation, has several bad years in a row. When it finally files for bankruptcy, it owes $50,000 to a number of suppliers and $80,000 as a result of a lawsuit for uninsured losses stemming from a fire. Stock in Rackafrax is owned by Harry Rack, Edith Frax, and John Quincy Taft. The personal assets of these owners cannot be taken to pay the money Rackafrax owes.

To protect yourself from personally having to pay business debts and claims, make a state filing to form one of the limited liability entities available to you under state law. All states allow you to create a limited liability company (LLC) or a corporation to obtain legal liability protection for all business owners. This means that your personal assets—such as your home, car, or individual bank account—will be beyond the reach of business creditors and claimants.

> **EXAMPLE 1:** Gizmos, a partnership owned by a married couple, retails high-priced specialty electronics toys and gadgets. Gizmos gets hit hard by a downturn in discretionary consumer spending and owes its creditors $70,000 when it finally goes under. Because the owners of a partnership are personally liable for business debts and claims, the spouses are personally liable for the shortfall, and they decide to file for personal bankruptcy to discharge the unpaid business debts. As part of the bankruptcy proceeding, the spouses hand over their nonexempt personal assets to the bankruptcy trustee to repay these debts.

EXAMPLE 2: Let's change the facts of the previous example and assume that the husband and wife formed Gizmos LLC, a limited liability company. When Gizmos LLC dissolves owing its creditors $70,000, the owners are not personally liable for any unpaid amount still owing after the assets of the LLC are tapped. The spouses do not need to file for personal bankruptcy nor liquidate and sell their personal assets to pay back the creditors of the business.

Exceptions to the Rule of Limited Personal Liability

In some unusual situations, corporate directors, officers, and shareholders can be required to pay money owed by their corporation or LLC. Here are a few of the most common exceptions to the rule of limited personal liability; these exceptions also apply to other limited liability business structures, such as the LLC.

- **Personal guarantees.** When a bank or other lender lends money to a small corporation, particularly a newly formed one, it often requires the principal corporate owners (shareholders) to agree to repay the loan from their personal assets if the corporation defaults. In some instances, shareholders may even have to pledge equity in a house or other personal assets as security for repayment of the debt.

- **Federal and state taxes.** If a corporation fails to pay income, payroll, or other taxes, the IRS and the state tax agency are likely to attempt to recover the unpaid taxes from "responsible persons"—a category that often includes the principal directors, officers, and shareholders of a small corporation. The IRS and state sometimes succeed in these tax collection strategies. Therefore, paying taxes should be a top priority for all businesses.

- **Unlawful or unauthorized transactions.** If you use the corporation as a means to defraud people, or if you intentionally make a reckless decision that results in physical harm to others or their property—for example, you fail to maintain premises or a worksite properly when you've been warned of the probability of imminent danger to others, or you manufacture products that you know to be unsafe—a court can hold you individually liable for the monetary losses of the people you harm. Lawyers call this "piercing the corporate veil," meaning that the corporate entity is disregarded and the owners are treated just like the owners of an unincorporated business. (See "Piercing the Veil," below.)

Fortunately, most of these problem areas can be avoided by following a few commonsense rules—rules you'll probably adhere to anyway. First, don't do anything dishonest or illegal. Second, make sure your corporation does the same, by obtaining necessary permits, licenses, or clearances for its business operations. Third, pay employee wages and withhold and pay corporate income and payroll taxes on time. Fourth, don't personally obligate yourself for corporate debts unless you decide that the need for corporate funds is worth the personal risk.

Here are some tips that will help you hold on to your limited liability protection:

- **Act fairly and legally.** Do not conceal or misrepresent material facts or the state of your finances to vendors, creditors, or other outsiders. Or, put more bluntly, don't engage in fraud.

- **Fund your LLC or corporation adequately.** You don't have to invest a lot of money in your LLC or corporation, but do try to start out with enough cash or other liquid assets to meet foreseeable expenses and liabilities. If you fail to do this, a court faced with a balance sheet that shows a very minimal investment may feel that you are playing fast and loose with your finances—and may disregard your limited liability protection if you have not fully disclosed your marginal financial situation to creditors, investors, and other outsiders who have a financial stake in your limited liability entity. This is particularly likely if you engage in a risky business that requires a large investment and you keep your marginal situation a secret.

Piercing the Veil

In some instances, courts will disregard an LLC's or corporation's separate legal status and hold its owners personally liable (in legal slang, this is called "piercing the corporate (or the LLC) veil"). Generally, the entity's limited liability protection will be disregarded if the owners fail to respect the separate legal existence of their LLC or corporation (they treat it as an extension of their personal affairs), and, as a result, creditors of the business are defrauded.

For example, a court may hold the owners liable if they paid their own personal bills from the entity's accounts without proper corporate or LLC authorization, leaving the business short of money to pay debts to outsiders. In a situation like this—where creditors were led to believe that the business was properly funded—a court is likely to say the LLC or corporation doesn't deserve its legal limited liability shield. Its owners are really doing business as individuals under a misleading corporate or LLC disguise and defrauding corporate creditors. In these extreme cases, the owners can be held personally liable for the business debts and claims of their LLC or corporation.

LLCs are legally allowed to act more informally than corporations (for example, under state law LLCs typically don't have to hold formal meetings), so the failure to adhere to these kinds of formalities should not be a problem for an LLC. A corporation's failure to hold meetings, in and of itself, shouldn't convince a court to pierce the corporate veil, unless there has been some fraud or extreme unfairness to outsiders.

- **Keep corporate/LLC and personal business separate.** Nothing will encourage a court to disrespect your limited-liability entity faster than your own failure to respect its status as an entity separate from its owners. This means you'll want to immediately get a federal Employer Identification Number and open up a separate business checking account. As a routine business practice, write all checks for business expenses or payouts of profits out of this account, and deposit all business revenue into it. Keep separate accounting books for your business—you can use a simple single-entry system, such as your check register and deposit slips, but a double-entry system will serve you better when it comes time to prepare your end-of-year income tax returns, especially if yours is a multimember company. Lastly, you should keep written records of all major business decisions. The best way is to make it a policy to hold corporate and LLC meetings to make all important business decisions, which are documented with written minutes placed in your LLC or corporate records book.

Limited Partnerships

A limited partnership (LP) also can be formed under state law, but only the investors in an LP get limited liability protection. The managing partners (there must be at least one in an LP) remain personally liable for business debts. Now that states allow the formation of LLCs, which give all owners—including all managers and investors—limited liability protection, LPs have fallen out of favor with entrepreneurs.

For these reasons, the LLC has become the entity of choice if the owners do not want to form a corporation. Forming an LLC provides a convenient and cheap form of liability insurance for unincorporated businesses—its limited liability protection provides an extra measure of personal liability protection over and above the limits of the business's commercial insurance policy.

Using Insurance to Limit Liability

INSURANCE, n. *An ingenious modern game of chance in which the player is permitted to enjoy the comfortable conviction that he is beating the man who keeps the table.*

—**Ambrose Bierce,** *The Devil's Dictionary*

Many businesses operate comfortably as sole proprietorships or partnerships because they have limited their liability in other ways. For example, you don't need to bother forming an LLC or a corporation if you avoid incurring substantial debts.

EXAMPLE: Sheila's Bowmakers receives an order for $300,000 worth of archery bows from SportCo, a sports equipment chain, to be paid on a net-90-days invoice. In order to fill this mammoth order, Sheila would have to buy $80,000 worth of supplies—and SportCo won't pay this cost in advance. Sheila decides not to accept the order, because she believes her business is not prepared to carry an $80,000 debt for three months. By doing this, she has reduced her personal liability (and reduced her need for the protection of a corporation or LLC), but she has also lost a valuable business opportunity.

One of the best ways to limit your liability—without limiting your business's potential for growth—is through insurance. Insurance can provide a suitable umbrella when creditor problems rain on your business. Although insurance coverage will add to your ongoing costs, the premiums will be regular and predictable.

EXAMPLE: Jack's retail collectible card business has sufficient insurance to cover injury to visitors, loss of business property, and any legal costs related to common business lawsuits. Because Jack's insurance covers most of the predictable disasters his business might face, there's probably no need for him to jump through the extra hoops required to form an LLC or corporation.

If forming a corporation or LLC can limit your liability, why bother with business insurance? Because the corporate or LLC form only protects you when your business goes under—that is, it's an endgame protection. If your business's debts become so burdensome that you must declare bankruptcy, having an LLC or corporate structure will shield you from personal loss. But until you cry "bankruptcy," your business must find a way to pay its debts—which, if you're uninsured, could leave you writing some hefty checks.

Insurance allows your business to take a licking and keep on ticking.

EXAMPLE 1: Leslie operates his collectible car business as an LLC. While Leslie is at a show, there's a fire in his studio, causing the loss of $90,000 in supplies and $30,000 in inventory. At the time of the fire, Leslie owes creditors about $45,000. Because he has an LLC, Leslie's business can declare bankruptcy and avoid paying the $45,000 in debts. His personal assets are unaffected. Still, his livelihood, his workspace, and his goodwill among suppliers (who are now wary of offering him credit) have all been damaged.

EXAMPLE 2: If Leslie had instead maintained fire insurance, he would receive compensation for his supplies and possibly rental costs for a temporary studio. He would be able to return to work—and eventually repay his creditors—without declaring bankruptcy.

Insurance has its drawbacks: periodic payments, annoying deductibles, and policy language that only a lawyer could love. But commercial and workers' compensation insurance is the best way to protect against business disasters such as fire, theft, injury to visitors, workplace injuries, and, if you can afford the extra premiums, injuries resulting from the use of your products or services, and even claims that you injured another business through false advertising. And if you are sued, your insurance policy may help pay not only your damages, but also the cost of hiring a lawyer to defend you (in fact, the insurance company will normally insist that you use their lawyers and agree to follow their advice concerning fighting or settling a lawsuit).

Sometimes your business *must* get insurance—for example, because state laws require you to obtain workers' compensation coverage, or because you sign a lease requiring you to have business and personal property coverage. In other cases, insurance may prove too expensive and you'll have to forgo it. A good insurance agent can help you make the right decisions about whether you need insurance and what type of coverage makes sense for your business.

Here are some tips on choosing and using your insurance wisely:

- Maintain enough property and liability coverage to protect yourself from common claims—for example, fire, theft, or accidental injury.

- Buy insurance against serious risks—that is, those that would cost you the most if they occurred (as long as the insurance is reasonably priced for your business).

- When possible, keep insurance costs down by selecting high deductibles.

- Do your best to reduce hazards or conditions that can lead to insurance claims.

Most businesses buy several kinds of insurance to protect them from business catastrophes:

- **Property insurance** covers damage to the space where you do business and to your business equipment—your computers, furnishings, inventory, and supplies. For example, if a fire destroys your studio, the insurance will cover the cost of restoring the studio and replacing your equipment and other tangible assets. Of course, you'll probably have to pay a deductible, and every policy places a cap on the total amount the insurance company will pay out.

- **Liability insurance** covers claims and lawsuits by people or businesses that have suffered physical or financial losses because of your business activities. This would include, for example, standard "slip-and-fall" coverage, which would handle a claim by a delivery person who trips on a cable in your office and breaks an ankle. As with property insurance, there may be a deductible for you to pay, and there will be a cap on your coverage.

TIP

If you have a full-business policy, consider adding an "in-transit" rider. Also known as an "inland marine" rider, this covers your inventory when it's in transit. The rider can cover replacement costs or costs arising from damage or theft that occurs while your inventory is away from your warehouse.

- **Business interruption insurance** covers losses you incur if you must temporarily curtail or cease operation because of a fire or flood. If your business property is damaged or destroyed, and you have to shut down for two months while your premises are rebuilt and your equipment is replaced, you may lose substantial income and have to pay significant expenses in the interim. These losses and expenses are covered by business interruption insurance.

Although your liability insurance may cover business legal disputes like defamation or copyright infringement, the policy language may be too narrow to include claims based on your website activities. Traditional policies lump defamation and copyright infringement claims into a category intended for *advertising* activities. Having a website may or may not be treated as advertising under your liability policy.

TIP

Pay attention to the amount of the deductible. The deductible is the portion of each claim that you're obligated to pay. By having a higher deductible, you can reduce the insurance premium. However, if you face an expensive claim or loss, you'll have to pay more money out of your own pocket before the insurance company starts chipping in.

Can the Personal Creditor of an LLC Owner Seize the Owner's LLC Interest?

The previous discussion about the LLC's limited liability shield dealt with how the law protects the personal, nonbusiness assets of LLC owners from lawsuits that arise from LLC business operations and claims. But can the personal creditor of an LLC owner seize the owner's interest in an LLC? Yes, under the laws of most states. Since an interest in an LLC is the personal property of each LLC owner, state law normally allows a creditor of an individual to obtain a charging order against that individual's interest in a business, such as a partnership or LLC interest or a person's stockholdings in a corporation. Essentially, a charging order represents a lien against the business interest, which allows the creditor to receive the payments of profits that would otherwise normally go to the owner of the interest.

EXAMPLE: Sam defaults on a personal bank loan unrelated to his LLC business, and the bank obtains a charging order against Sam's LLC membership interest. This order allows the bank to be paid any profits that are distributed to Sam under the terms of the LLC's operating agreement.

Can the Personal Creditor of an LLC Owner
Seize the Owner's LLC Interest? (cont'd)

A charging order may not do a creditor much good if an LLC does not regularly distribute profits to members. In that case, a creditor may be able to ask a state court to foreclose on the LLC's member's interest. If the state's laws allow this foreclosure, and if the court agrees, a personal creditor of an LLC member can become the new legal owner of the LLC. However, under most state laws, the creditor who forecloses on an LLC interest does not become a full owner. Instead, the law says that the foreclosing creditor becomes a "transferee" or "assignee" who is entitled to all economic rights associated with the interest—such as a share of the profits paid out on the interest as well as the value of the interest when the business is sold or liquidated. Typically an assignee or transferee is not allowed to manage or vote in the LLC nor assume other membership rights granted to full members under the LLC operating agreement.

Forming and Running Your Business

The Latin word *forma* refers to shape or structure. This chapter uses three variations on this word—form, formation, and formalities—to analyze the relative ease (or difficulty) of creating and running each type of business entity. Let's look at each of these words, briefly:

- "Form" (as a noun) refers to the type of business structure, such as a corporation or LLC—for example, "I have chosen a corporation as my business form." "Form" (as a verb) refers to how you create your business entity—for example, "I formed an LLC."

- "Formation" comprises the processes and methods for creating the specific business entities.

- "Formalities" are the government regulations and legal rules that you must abide by when forming and running your business—for example, in order to create an LLC, you must file articles of organization with the state business entity filing office.

This chapter examines the formalities you'll have to follow during the formation process for each business form—that is, it explains the steps you'll have to take to start up and run each type of business entity.

Forming and Running a Sole Proprietorship

Eighty percent of the businesses in the United States are sole proprietorships—and it's easy to see why they're so popular. Forming and running one is effortless. All you have to do is sell your goods or services. If you're running your business by yourself—that is, without anyone sharing the expenses and profits—and you haven't formed an LLC or a corporation, you've already created a sole proprietorship.

Who's Your Agent?

In legalese, an agent is someone who is legally authorized to act on behalf of a business—for example, to enter into a verbal or written contract, or agree to a particular course of action. Because agency rules vary from one type of business to another, you should make sure that you are comfortable with the agency rules that apply to the entity you want to form. In other words, make sure you know who can legally speak for your business and commit it to a contract or course of action with someone outside the business, such as a supplier, financial institution, government agency, and the like. Here are the basic agency rules:

- **Sole proprietorship.** The sole owner is the agent of the business and can act for it.
- **General partnership.** Each partner can manage the business, and each is empowered to act as an agent of the business. This means that each owner can enter into contracts and pursue a course of conduct that legally binds the partnership.
- **Limited partnership.** Only the general partners who manage the business have authority to speak for and bind the partnership. Normally, the limited partner investors do not have legal authority to manage or bind the business as its agent.
- **LLC.** In a member-managed LLC where all members manage the business, most states give each member (owner) the right to act as an agent of the business. In a manager-managed LLC, only the managers can act as agents.
- **Corporation.** Officers usually act as agents of the corporation and commit it to contracts and business deals. Corporate law generally allows a third party (an outsider to a business) to assume that an officer or other supervisory employee of a corporation has the authority to bind the corporation unless the outsider actually knows otherwise (usually because he or she has been told that the officer cannot bind the corporation). This concept is called "apparent authority" and generally means that outsiders can enforce contracts and deals made with the corporate officers—even if these officers are not specifically authorized to act for the corporation.

Paperwork Required for All Businesses

If you're starting a new business from scratch, you'll have to take care of some paperwork, no matter what business form you choose. Most businesses will need to obtain one or more of the following:

- **EIN.** An Employer Identification Number (EIN) is generally required for partnerships, co-owned LLCs, all corporations, and, under some circumstances, sole proprietors. If you are a sole proprietor without employees, or a one-owner LLC without employees, you can use your Social Security number for preparing your income tax returns, opening up a bank account, and most other tax chores. However, a sole proprietorship or a one-owner LLC must have an EIN if it has employees or if it sets up a qualified retirement plan, such as a Keogh (HR-10) plan; an EIN is necessary to prepare employment tax as well as retirement plan returns with the IRS. To obtain an EIN, complete IRS Form SS-4, *Application for Employer Identification Number.* (You can download it from the IRS website at www.irs.gov.) You may also fill in the form and file for an EIN via the Internet at the IRS website, or by calling a toll-free number: 800-829-4933.

- **DBA.** If you're doing business under an assumed name, most local governments require you to file a DBA ("doing business as") statement. You can find out the details from the county clerk at your local courthouse. If you're doing business under your own name (that is, your last name—for example, *Wellhausen's Welding Studio*), you won't need to file. Registering your business name as a DBA with your county clerk or filing incorporation papers does not guarantee your right to use your name in business or to identify your products. Before choosing a name for your business, you may need to review legal rules regarding trade names and trademarks.

- **Local Permits.** In addition to filing a DBA, your local or state government may have other permit or licensing requirements. You can usually find out the details at your county clerk's office.

Forming a Sole Proprietorship

Starting a sole proprietorship requires little more than hanging out a sign or shingle or opening a storefront. This is the primary convenience associated with creating sole proprietorships as compared to LLCs and corporations—you don't have to make a formal filing with the state to start up your business.

Although a sole proprietorship is easy to form, you will still have to meet some obligations—for example, income taxes, sales taxes, payroll taxes—to keep the business running. In addition, regardless of how casually you start your sole proprietorship, you may need or want to meet certain formalities, depending on the type of business. (See "Paperwork Required for All Businesses," above.)

Running a Sole Proprietorship

For those in business, the ultimate freedom and independence comes from running a sole proprietorship. You can make business decisions as you wish, without consulting investors, managers, members, or partners. As a sole proprietor, all you have to do to keep your business afloat is use basic bookkeeping principles; abide by the tax laws; and obey any other municipal, state, or federal government rules that are specific to your enterprise—for example, laws regarding the sale of fireworks, food services, or limousine services. Unlike corporations and LLCs, there are no laws or formalities that dictate how you must manage your sole proprietorship; there are no required annual meetings, filings, or record-keeping requirements (other than those described above; see "Paperwork Required for All Businesses").

Forming and Running a Partnership

For most partnerships, the legal side of forming and running the business is similar to sole proprietorships: a lot of freedom and few legal restrictions. Like a sole proprietorship, a partnership need only follow established accounting principles, abide by the tax laws, and obey laws specific to your enterprise. However, there are a few additional issues to consider when forming and running a general partnership.

Forming a Partnership

To create a partnership (also known as a general partnership), you don't have to do anything other than start your business with one or more other people. A general partnership has no formalities—that is, you don't have to file formal paperwork or pay fees to the state to formalize its status. In short, partners can simply start doing business.

TIP
You must file paperwork with the state to form an LP or RLLP.
Although you don't have to file any paperwork to form a general partnership, you will have to file forms with your state to create a limited partnership (LP) or a registered limited liability partnership (RLLP). To find out what requirements you will have to meet to form one of these entities in your state, go to your state's corporate filing office website, which also handles LP and RLLP filings. (See the appendix.)

The only problem with this let's-get-together-and-start-a-business approach is that unless the partners have a written agreement, certain partnership obligations and rules can be unclear. For example:

- How much money, property, or services does each partner pay into the partnership to get it started?
- Who will work for the partnership?
- How will profits and losses be divided and paid out to the partners?

- What happens if the partners split up—who buys the other person(s) out, and for how much?
- What happens if a partner dies?
- If the partnership folds, who gets to use the name in a new business?

If the partners get in a dispute and they have not prepared a written agreement, the default provisions of state partnership law may decide some or all of these issues for them—and the legal result may not be to their liking.

That's why every partnership should have a written agreement establishing each partner's share of the income and setting out what will happen if one partner leaves or dies.

RESOURCE
For more information on forming a partnership and creating a partnership agreement, read *Form a Partnership,* by Denis Clifford and Ralph Warner (Nolo). Or check out Nolo's website (www.nolo.com), where you can learn more about partnerships and also purchase and download a partnership form agreement with explanations.

Running a Partnership

Running a sole proprietorship has its benefits—including the freedom to make decisions alone and to keep all the profits—but it also has its disadvantages: There's nobody to help run the show or to share the expenses and work.

Although there are no statutory formalities for running a partnership —for example, no state laws dictate how decisions must be made or how the partners must vote on matters—the truth is that you can't always do what you want in a partnership, because your actions and decisions affect the other partners. And because the general partners can be liable for the actions of the other general partners, running a partnership can get a bit complicated.

EXAMPLE: Allen has run a successful audio-production business for several years. He decides to take on a partner, Phoebe, a recording engineer who will bring her skills—and her expensive recording equipment—to the partnership. Phoebe has no experience running a business, and Allen is concerned that she will make decisions that could affect his personal liability and his relationship with the clients. He enters into a partnership agreement with Phoebe that details who will make certain decisions and how the two of them will vote on others.

When it comes to making important decisions, it's always wise to talk things over with all the partners and respect each other's opinions. But achieving unanimity on everything can be hard—which makes it impractical to choose unanimity as a standard for decision making. A majority vote on routine decisions allows you more flexibility and probably won't cause any serious disputes. Most partnerships require unanimity only on major business decisions such as adding a new partner or closing down the business. You can specify these standards and rules in your partnership agreement.

Similarly, your agreement can establish guidelines for other issues, such as what happens when one partner leaves, where the partnership records are kept and who maintains them, what happens when you want to add a new partner, what happens if a partner dies, and how you value each partner's contributions.

Of course, creating a partnership agreement is no guarantee that the partnership will run smoothly. The reality is that for a small partnership to succeed, the partners need to have shared goals and confidence in one another's judgment. If those elements don't exist, a partnership agreement won't help, no matter how detailed it is. Put more bluntly, if you don't trust your partners and enjoy working with them, don't bother creating a partnership in the first place.

> **TIP**
> **Both spouses should sign business start-up agreements.**
> Because state law may give a nonowner spouse an interest in a business
> owned and operated by the other spouse, the original owners of a business
> should ask each married owner to have his or her spouse sign any charter
> agreements signed by the owners, such as an LLC operating agreement,
> partnership agreement, or corporate shareholders' agreement. This can
> help avoid problems later, if the spouses divorce and the nonowner spouse
> receives some or all of the owner spouse's interest in the business as part of
> a property settlement in the divorce proceeding. For example, a nonowner
> spouse may want to step into the shoes of the owner-spouse and help
> manage the business or may wish to get some quick cash by selling the
> interest to an outsider. The business agreement may seek to prevent these
> results—for example, by prohibiting transfers except to the current owners
> at a set price or only after the other owners are given a right of first refusal
> to buy the interest back. Or perhaps the agreement permits new owners
> to obtain only economic rights (rights to profits), not the voting rights
> associated with the business interest. If the nonowner spouse signed the
> original business agreement, the other owners stand a good chance of
> requiring him or her to abide by its terms.

Forming and Running a Limited Liability Company

In many ways, the LLC is the business entity that gets it right for the
small business owner. It eliminates the downside of sole proprietorships
and partnerships—personal liability for business debts and claims—but
it keeps the upside—pass-through taxation rules. And an LLC is also
fairly easy to form and run.

Is It Time to Form an LLC?

Many entrepreneurs feel that forming an LLC is so simple and inexpensive—and provides a comfortable level of personal insurance against legal claims—that it is the best way to do business right from the start. Others decide to do business informally as a sole proprietor or partnership first, then ease their way into an LLC once they feel more certain that their business has a good chance of success.

Only you can decide if and when it makes sense to take the time and trouble to form an LLC—there's no one correct approach. It depends on your type of business, how comfortable you are with risk, whether you feel the need to limit your personal liability, and your willingness to take on the required paperwork and fees, among other things. Chapters 6 and 7 explain how to convert your business from a sole proprietorship or partnership to an LLC.

Forming an LLC

To form an LLC, you'll have to fill out some paperwork and pay filing fees. You must prepare and file articles of organization and pay a filing fee with the secretary of state's office. Once your articles are filed, your LLC is an official legal entity, and its limited liability protection kicks in to shelter your personal assets from business creditors.

It shouldn't take too long—or cost too much—to file LLC articles. The articles must include standard bits of information, such as the name and address of the entity and how and by whom it will be managed. State fees for filing articles typically average $100 or less. (You can view the LLC filing fees at the website for your state's business filing office; see the appendix.)

However, just like partners in a partnership, LLC owners should do more than just the minimum required paperwork. LLC owners should prepare an LLC operating agreement—a document similar to a partnership agreement, which defines the rights, responsibilities, and relationship among the owners. And while LLCs are not legally required to hold meetings, it makes sense for LLC managers and members to meet when they have to make and document important LLC legal, tax, or business decisions.

When you're trying to choose the right business entity, you should consider how many owners you expect in your business. You can form an LLC with only one owner (called a "member" in the LLC statutes) in all states; LLCs can also work fine with small numbers of owners. However, an LLC becomes top-heavy and unwieldy if there are too many cooks in the kitchen (managers) or investors in the capital contribution pool. If you plan to have more than 35 owners, it may be better to organize your business as a corporation.

RELATED TOPIC

Want help forming your LLC? In the final section of this chapter, resources are provided to help small business entrepreneurs prepare and file articles of organization and complete the other paperwork associated with organizing an LLC (or a corporation).

TIP

Securities laws favor businesses with 35 or fewer investors. Federal and most state securities laws treat 35 as a "magic" number—if you have 35 or fewer investors, your LLC probably will be exempt from security registration filings and fees for private sales of business ownership interests, such as issuing LLC memberships or corporate stock.

Check Out State LLC Annual Fees Before Forming an LLC

In most states, LLCs are not charged a separate entity-level tax, or, if they are, such taxes normally are more modest in amount and are calculated on actual net income (profits) earned by the LLC. You can view information on LLC annual taxes at your state's business filing website. (See the appendix.) In some states, like California, for example, the fees are based on the value of goods "consumed" and can become exorbitant. Consider the following example under California's statutory LLC fee scheme.

EXAMPLE: Antoine is a successful sculptor who is regularly commissioned by governmental and nonprofit agencies to produce original works for installation in parks and buildings throughout the United States. On his lawyer's advice, Antoine formed an LLC, Heavy Metal Ltd. Liability Co., to help protect him from personal liability for lawsuits.

California requires the payment of a minimum $800 LLC tax each year. California also requires the payment of an additional LLC fee depending on LLC gross receipts. Unfortunately, what Antoine and his lawyer did not know was that the worksheet that is used to calculate the LLC's gross receipts requires that the LLC's cost of goods—in Antoine's business, this means the price he pays for his materials—is included in his total LLC annual receipts. At the end of the first LLC tax year, Antoine had paid $300,000 for materials he needed to produce his currently commissioned work.

He had been paid the funds to buy the materials by the client, but he had not yet received any other payments under the commission contract. So, not surprisingly, Antoine was not pleased when his bookkeeper calculated his annual LLC gross receipts fee at $900, which he had to pay in addition to the regular $800 annual LLC tax, for a total of $1,700—even though Heavy Metal had not received any net profits under the contract. Antoine called his lawyer and asked him to immediately dissolve his LLC—he told her that he'd prefer to go back to producing sculptures as a sole proprietorship and take his chances in court with dissatisfied clients rather than have to pay taxes to the state on materials used in his business.

Running an LLC

LLCs are a good choice for small businesses operated by a close-knit group of people who want the freedom to run their business as they see fit—and to change the rules as they go along (with the consent of all owners, of course).

State LLC laws set up very basic ground rules for running an LLC, but these rules act only as defaults. In other words, most of these rules apply only if you don't create your own rule on the same topic in your LLC's articles or operating agreement.

The default rules in a state LLC act may say:

- that the LLC will be managed by all members

- that each member will have a right to LLC profits, voting rights, and LLC assets (if the LLC is liquidated) according to the value of each member's capital contributions to the LLC, and

- that LLC membership interests cannot be transferred nor new memberships issued without the consent of all members.

These default rules may work just fine for many smaller LLCs. However, many state LLC statutes don't address a host of other important matters. This means that you may have to create your own rules on issues like:

- when distributions of profits will be made to members and the amount of such distributions

- whether members will be required to invest additional capital after their initial contributions, and what will happen if a member does not make a required contribution

- how the capital accounts of each member (the financial accounts tracking each owner's interest in the business) will be maintained and adjusted during the life of the LLC, and

- whether a member is entitled to be bought out upon leaving the LLC—and, if so, how the buyout amount will be calculated.

State LLC acts also give you the right to decide who will manage the business. The default rule in most states is that all members (owners) manage the LLC unless the articles or LLC operating agreement selects manager-management. Under a member-managed arrangement, every member of an LLC has a say in how the business is run and every member can sign agreements binding the LLC (unless otherwise prohibited by agreement). Manager-managed LLCs are managed by a specially designated manager or managers—and these can be members or nonmembers. This allows you to delegate management responsibilities—and limit the number of people authorized to speak for the LLC—to a smaller group.

> EXAMPLE: Chester and Lester are the sole members of Pluck and Bow, LLC, a music performance and publishing company. They are expert acoustic guitar, mandolin, and fiddle players who hire themselves out—as employees of their own LLC—for soundtrack and studio sessions with major music labels and film production companies. They also publish their own sheet music and record and sell acoustic instrumental music CDs under their "Unplugged Pluck" label. Their original LLC is member-managed; each performer is an agent of the LLC and can book the duo for performances and studio sessions. Business picks up, and the duo bring in additional musicians as songwriting collaborators and performers. Chester and Lester change the business structure to a manager-managed LLC. Under their new operating agreement, Chester and Lester are the sole managers of the LLC. New musicians are brought in as minority members (owners) and employees, but they cannot book shows or sign contracts.

Because state LLC rules are sparse—and even when they exist, they may not be the best solution for a particular LLC—the best way to run your LLC is to spell out your own rules in an LLC operating agreement.

When an LLC Loses Members

Normally the loss of an LLC member will have little effect on an LLC in which several members remain, provided that the LLC operating agreement deals with this contingency. The LLC members can, for example, agree in their operating agreement that the LLC will legally dissolve when one of the members leaves, but dissolution is not required and such a contingency is rare.

Things can become more complicated when an LLC is left with only one member. Unlike a partnership, which terminates legally and is automatically converted into a sole proprietorship when it is left with just one owner, a co-owned LLC does not, as a matter of law, automatically terminate and change into a sole proprietorship when it is left with just one member. Again, the operating agreement may provide for dissolution in this situation, but, usually, the LLC remains intact and operates as a one-person LLC.

An exception to this rule is Wyoming, where a two-member LLC will dissolve legally when it is left with just one member unless the LLC has elected to become a "flexible limited liability company" in its articles. (Check the appendix to find the Wyoming filing office website and to learn more about the Wyoming flexible limited liability company rules.)

However, there may be a significant change in tax status if a multimember LLC becomes a one-member LLC, since the LLC's partnership tax status will terminate and the LLC will then be taxed as the sole proprietorship of the remaining LLC owner. In other words, the technical tax termination of a partnership entity (such as a multi-member LLC) can involve significant tax costs.

Of course, in any state, if a one-member LLC loses its last member, through death, disability, withdrawal of the member, or otherwise, the LLC will automatically dissolve since, under state law, an LLC must have at least one member. The mechanics of the dissolution when a one-member LLC dissolves vary from state to state, but states normally give an LLC some time after the loss of the last member of an LLC to find a new member before a legal dissolution of the LLC occurs.

Forming and Running a Corporation

The best known liability shield is the modern corporation—a business entity that has provided a haven for investors and businesspeople for centuries and has enjoyed enormous advantages under tax law. (In the 1980s, for example, 50 of America's biggest corporations did not pay any federal income tax.) But is incorporating the right choice for you? This section explains what's required to form and run a corporation.

Forming a Corporation

You'll have to fill out some paperwork and pay a filing fee to form your corporation. Corporate liability protection and tax benefits commence as soon as you file articles of incorporation and pay your fee. The articles contain basic information about the corporation, including its name and address, how and by whom it will be managed, and the number and type of shares it will issue to start. Smaller corporations often designate one class of common stock; all such shares will have equal voting, dividend, and liquidation rights. State fees for filing corporate articles typically average $100 or less. For more information on corporation filing fees in your state, see your state's business filing office website. (See the appendix.)

Corporation owners should do more than just the minimum required paperwork, however. Corporate founders should also prepare bylaws explaining the duties and responsibilities of corporate directors (managers), owners (shareholders), and officers. Annual meetings of directors and shareholders, which are required in most states, should also be scheduled in the bylaws.

You can form a corporation with only one owner (shareholder) under the laws of every state. Further, in many states, one person can serve as both the sole shareholder and the sole director of the corporation. In many states, the same person also can fill all required officer positions (many states require corporations to have a president, treasurer, and secretary). In other words, most states allow you to form a one-person corporation.

A handful of states require you to designate two separate people to fill the corporate officer positions of president and secretary, respectively. (If a married couple runs the corporation, each spouse can fill one of these officer positions if the state requires the positions to be held by two different people.) Some states require a minimum number of directors based on the number of corporate shareholders: If you have two shareholders, you must have two directors, and if you have three or more shareholders, you need at least three directors in these states. For more information on your state's corporate director and officer requirements, see your state's business filing office website. (See the appendix.)

> ⓘ **CAUTION**
> **Other businesses cannot be corporate directors.** Corporate directors must be individuals; unlike LLCs, a corporation cannot have another corporation, LLC, or other type of business entity serve as a manager (director) of the corporation.

Running a Corporation

If you want to run a business in which the roles of manager and investor are separated under state laws, then the corporation may be an ideal choice. When you form a corporation, you immediately inherit the basic statutory ground rules contained in your state corporation act, which defines separate rights and responsibilities for managers (directors), owners or investors (shareholders), day-to-day supervisors (officers), and regular employees.

In a corporation, the directors make high-level policy and management decisions at annual (or more frequent) board of directors meetings, and they delegate the implementation of these broad decisions to the officers of the corporation. In addition, certain officers have specific statutory duties—for example, under state corporation act provisions, the president of the corporation may be responsible for chairing board meetings; the treasurer or chief financial officer may be charged with making sure that annual financial records are prepared and mailed to shareholders; and the secretary typically is responsible for ensuring that director and shareholder meetings are properly called, held, and recorded in the corporate records.

Each state's corporation act includes rules about:

• how shares are issued and paid for

• what rights and restrictions may be imposed upon shares

• how and when the corporation may make distributions to shareholders

• how often meetings of directors and shareholders must be held, and

• when and how a corporation must seek shareholder approval to sell its assets, merge with another corporation, or dissolve.

State laws also contain additional rules that govern various aspects of corporate formation, operation, and termination. This collection of corporate rules, formalities, and designated responsibilities is one of the built-in benefits of forming a corporation.

EXAMPLE: Myra, Danielle, and Rocco form a three-person corporation, Skate City, Incorporated, a skate and bike shop in Venice Beach, California. Storefront access to the Venice Beach roller blade, skating, and bike path makes it popular with local roller bladers and bicyclists. Needing more cash, the three owners approach relatives for investment capital. Rocco's brother, Tony, and Danielle's sister, Colette, chip in $10,000 each in return for shares in the business. Myra's Aunt Kate lends the corporation $25,000 in return for an interest-only promissory note, with the principal amount to be repaid at the end of five years. Here's how the management, executive, and financial structure of this small corporation breaks down.

Board of directors. The management team, which meets once each quarter to analyze and project financial performance and review store operations, consists of the three founders, Myra, Danielle, and Rocco, and one of the other three investors. The investor board position is a one-year rotating seat. This year Tony has the investor board seat; next year, Colette; the third year, Aunt Kate. This pattern repeats every three years. Directors have one vote apiece, regardless of share ownership—this means that the founders can always outvote the investor vote on the board, but it also guarantees that each of the investors will have an opportunity to hear board discussions and give input on major management decisions.

Executive officer team. The officers or executive team charged with overseeing day-to-day business; supervising employees; keeping track of ordering, inventory, and sales activities; and generally putting into practice the goals set by the board are Myra (President) and Danielle (Vice President). Rocco fills the remaining officer positions of Secretary/Treasurer of the corporation, but this is a part-time administrative task only. Rocco's real vocation—or avocation—is blading along the beach and training to be a professional touring roller blader with his own corporate sponsor (maybe Skate City if profits continue to roll in).

Participation in profits. Corporate net profits are used to buy inventory, pay rent on the Venice Beach storefront, and fund all the other usual and customary expenses of doing business. The two full-time executives, Myra and Danielle, get a corporate salary, plus a year-end bonus when profits are good. Rocco gets a small stipend (hourly pay) for his part-time work. Otherwise, he and the two investor shareholders are simply sitting on their shares. Skate City is not in a position yet to pay dividends—all of the corporation's excess profits are used to continue expanding the store's product lines and add a new service facility at the back of the store. Even if dividends are never paid, all three know that their stock will increase in value if the business is successful. They can cash in their shares when the business sells or when they decide to sell their shares back to the corporation. Aunt Kate, the most conservative investor, will receive ongoing interest payments as her share of corporate profits, getting her capital back when the principal amount of her loan is repaid.

In the example above, the state corporation statute automatically defines the basic rights and responsibilities of Skate City's directors, officers, and shareholders. The founders need only fill in a few blanks on a standard state articles of incorporation form, fill in blanks in standard corporate bylaws, prepare standard organization meeting minutes, fill in and distribute stock certificates, and prepare a standard promissory note for Aunt Kate. To duplicate this structure, an LLC would need a specially drafted LLC operating agreement with custom language, reviewed by the founders and investors (and, no doubt, their lawyers).

Resources for Forming an LLC or Corporation

The prospect of forming an LLC or corporation can be exciting, but many people find the legal paperwork less than thrilling. Fortunately, there are plenty of resources available to you to help you handle most or all of the legal paperwork necessary to form your own LLC or corporation. This section reviews several of the most helpful resources.

State Websites

Each state has an office that accepts LLC and corporate filings—and each of these offices maintains a website on the Internet. You can find your state's business entity filing website using the resources in the appendix.

Most states provide fill-in-the-blanks standard articles to form LLCs and corporations. Download the form, fill it in on your computer according to the instructions provided with the form, then print and mail the form together with the required filing fee to the office for filing. The turnaround time in most states to process and file articles is one to two weeks.

States are also starting to provide online articles filing services. If your state provides this service, just fill in the articles form within your browser, then submit the form for filing (you don't have to print and mail the form to the office). The filing fee is charged to your credit card. Typically, online filing is accomplished on the same day or within a few days, and you'll receive a filing receipt from the office within a week of the submission date.

Legal and Business Self-Help Books

Some business organizers may prefer to learn more about the basic legal and tax issues surrounding business formation before they prepare the forms to create their business entity. The fact that you are reading this book means that you are probably one of these people.

There are several commercial publishers of books and software that provide background information on LLCs and corporations, plus the necessary forms to organize your own business entity. Nolo (800-728-3555; www.nolo.com), the publisher of this book, is a leading, user-friendly source of self-help business formation and operation books and software as well as providing filing services for LLCs and corporations. Below is a partial list from their catalog of business entity formation and operation resources (see additional Nolo catalog and ordering information at the back of this book).

- *Form Your Own Limited Liability Company*, by Anthony Mancuso. This national title shows you how to form this newest type of business entity under each state's LLC law and the latest federal rules. Includes instructions for preparing articles of organization plus CD-ROM operating agreements for member-managed and manager-managed LLCs.

- *Your Limited Liability Company: An Operating Manual*, by Anthony Mancuso. This book with CD-ROM provides ready-to-use minutes forms for holding formal LLC meetings; it also contains resolutions to insert in your minutes to formally approve standard legal, tax, and other important business decisions that arise in the course of operating an LLC.

- *Incorporate Your Business,* by Anthony Mancuso. This book explains how to form a corporation, with instructions for preparing articles and CD-ROM bylaws and organizational minutes. Includes comprehensive state-by-state corporate, tax, and securities law information. (If you plan to form a California corporation, see *How to Form Your Own California Corporation,* also by Anthony Mancuso.)

- *The Corporate Records Handbook,* by Anthony Mancuso. This book shows you how to hold and document ongoing corporate meetings of your board and shareholders. It also contains more than 80 corporate resolutions to insert in your minutes to handle common legal, tax, and business transactions that occur after incorporating. The book comes with legal forms on an enclosed CD-ROM and as tear-outs.

- *Form a Partnership,* by Denis Clifford and Ralph Warner. Step-by-step instructions for preparing your own partnership agreement. Plenty of helpful, down-to-earth examples and practical insights to help you assemble the best agreement for your partnership. Includes tear-out and CD-ROM forms.

- *The Small Business Start-Up Kit,* by Peri H. Pakroo, J.D. A great resource that explains the basic nuts and bolts of getting an unincorporated business off the ground, including business and employer registration requirements, basic single-entry bookkeeping procedures, tax reporting information, commercial insurance information, and plenty more.

- *Legal Guide for Starting & Running a Small Business*, by Fred S. Steingold. This book is an excellent general legal transaction resource for the small business owner. Find out how to negotiate a favorable lease, hire and fire employees, write contracts, and resolve business disputes.

- *Tax Savvy for Small Business*, by Frederick W. Daily. This book gives business owners basic information they need about federal taxes and shows them how to make the best tax decisions for their business, maximize their profits, and stay out of trouble with the IRS.

- *How to Write a Business Plan*, by Mike McKeever. If you're thinking of starting a business or raising money to expand an existing one, this book will show you how to write the business plan and loan package necessary to finance your business and make it work. Includes up-to-date sources of financing. ●

Money Issues: Taxes, Profits, Losses, and Investments

What financial goals do you hope to accomplish with your business entity? Of course, you'd probably like to earn as much and keep as much of what you earn as possible. But have you considered how you will achieve these goals? For example, do you see yourself distributing profits at the end of each year, or do you plan to leave the profits in the business to fund future growth? Do you envision private or institutional investments, or do you plan to be the sole owner and investor?

The business form you choose will determine which financial options are available to you. For example, if you dream of an initial public offering, you eventually will have to convert your sole proprietorship, partnership, or LLC into a corporation. Your choice of business entity will affect:

• how your business is taxed

• how your profits are treated

• how investments are handled, and

• how losses are managed.

This chapter will help you compare how each type of entity deals with money and financial issues. (Much of the advice in this chapter, particularly the tax analysis, will reappear in subsequent chapters on converting from one type of entity to another.)

Taxes

To understand how money flows through your business, you must first look at the rules that the IRS and state tax agencies use to classify and tax different business entities and their owners. These rules create a default tax treatment for each type of business entity, but they also allow business owners to change the tax classification of their business. Knowing these rules will help you select the proper business entity: the business form that gives you the most favorable tax treatment for your situation and, if you are looking forward to the prospect of growing your business, the flexibility to convert to another type of business entity without running up a hefty tax bill.

Under federal and state tax rules, there are two types of business income tax treatment:

• pass-though treatment, and

• corporate tax treatment.

As you would expect, corporations get corporate tax treatment as a default; all other business forms are treated as pass-through entities.

Pass-Through Tax Treatment

If your business has pass-through tax treatment, as sole proprietorships, partnerships, and LLCs do by default, you will report and pay tax on your business profits on your individual income tax return. These profits are taxed even if they are kept in the business and not actually paid out to the owners. For example, if your partnership or LLC earns $100,000, the owner(s) will pay taxes on that amount, whether or not they actually receive the money.

Many small business owners like the simplicity of pass-through tax treatment, because it allows them to report and pay taxes on business profits once, on their personal income tax returns. The owners know that they will pay taxes on all profits each year, so they do not have to decide how much money to pay themselves and how much to keep in the business, nor do they have to deal with the other issues and complexities that pop up in the corporate tax world.

Sole Proprietorships and Partnerships

Sole proprietorships and partnerships provide pass-through treatment with one level of income taxation to the owners. A sole proprietor reports business profits and losses on Schedule C, *Profit or Loss From Business*; a partnership files a Form 1065 Schedule K-1, *Partner's Share of Income, Deductions, Credits, etc.*

EXAMPLE: Willy's Widget Works is an unincorporated foundry that produces custom metal fixtures and structures for industrial applications and state and federal government work projects. In its early years, WWW is owned and operated solely by Willy. Each year, Willy files a 1040 federal income tax return and reports his income and expenses on 1040 Schedule C, *Profit or Loss From Business*. He pays individual income taxes on his net profits. He also pays self-employment (Social Security and Medicare) taxes, which are based upon his Schedule C net profits and calculated on 1040 Form SE.

After a few years, Willy decides to expand and bring in two other welders as new co-owners. The three agree to share the workload, expenses, and profits. Thereafter, WWW files an annual IRS Form 1065, *U.S. Return of Partnership Income*, and gives each owner a 1065 Schedule K-1, *Partner's Share of Income, Deductions, Credits etc.*, which shows the amount of income or loss, deductions, credits, and other items each will report on his or her individual 1040 tax return. Because the owners are all active in the business, each also reports his or her share of net profits on Form SE and pays self-employment tax on that amount.

LLCs

Although sole proprietorships and partnerships offer tax simplicity, they also have a major disadvantage: The owners of the business are personally liable for its debts. Even a limited partnership, which also provides pass-through taxation of business profits, is required to have one general partner who is personally liable for its debts. For that reason, many businesses that want pass-through taxation and limited personal liability choose to form a limited liability company (LLC).

The IRS treats a one-owner LLC just like a sole proprietorship for purposes of income tax reporting and payment; a multiowner LLC is treated like a partnership. There are no special LLC federal tax forms; the LLC simply uses the same forms a sole proprietorship or partnership would use to report its profits. This means that an existing sole proprietorship or partnership can convert to an LLC to obtain the legal benefits of limited liability protection without any change in its IRS income tax reporting requirements.

And, because the IRS has ruled that the act of converting a sole proprietorship or partnership to an LLC is normally not a taxable event, usually you will not owe taxes solely because of the conversion (as you would if you sold the assets and liabilities of a sole proprietorship or partnership to an existing business entity). For more information on the tax treatment of converting a partnership to an LLC, see Chapter 7.

EXAMPLE: The three owners of Willy's Widget Works (WWW) are sued by the state highway commission for damages resulting from the collapse of a highway overpass pillar allegedly caused by WWW's poor craftsmanship. The partners are sure that the pillar collapse was not their fault, but they can't afford the time or money it would take to perform their own investigation and fight the state in court. WWW settles the case and then converts the partnership to a limited liability company (LLC) to make sure that the owners' personal assets are sheltered from claims or creditors in the future. Because multimember LLCs are treated by the IRS as partnerships, WWW does not need to change it tax filings at the end of the next tax year. After it converts to an LLC, WWW continues to file its 1065 partnership return.

How Do You Keep Track of Your Tax Basis?

In a pass-through tax entity, such as an LLC, partnership, or S corporation, once profits have been allocated and taxed to an owner, they can be paid out to the owner later, tax-free. This is, of course, the premise of pass-through taxation—just one level of taxation.

But if an LLC has cash reserves and decides to pay $10,000 to each owner, how does each owner know how much of the $10,000 has already been allocated and taxed to the owner in prior years? Does the owner have to backtrack though years of past financial statements or tax returns of the LLC or partnership to see if $10,000 has already been allocated and taxed but not paid out to the owner? No, each owner of the business has an income tax *basis*: a tax system that tracks the amount of profits already allocated and taxed to an owner, but not paid out.

Here's how it works:

1. An owner's income tax basis in a partnership, LLC, or S corporation (simply called "basis") is increased by the amount of cash or the existing basis of property paid into the business by the owner as a capital contribution.

2. The basis is increased (or reduced) each year by the amount of profits (or loss) allocated to each owner. Each owner pays income taxes on allocated profits at the end of each year (whether or not they are paid out to the owner).

3. The basis is reduced by the amount of any actual distribution of cash (or fair market value of any property) paid out to the owners.

4. The basis is increased by the amount of entity-level debt: money owed by the LLC. Conversely, the basis is reduced when an owner is relieved of a portion of entity-level debt—for example, when an LLC liability allocated among the owners is paid off by the LLC. Generally, in an LLC or general partnership, business liabilities are allocated among all the owners (technical rules determine the percentage of allocation to each owner).

5. Whenever a downward adjustment is made to the basis, it is not allowed to go below zero (the downward adjustment stops at zero).

Here is an example that shows how the basis adjustment rules are designed to keep track of the amount of profits that have already been allocated and taxed to an owner, so that an owner can use his or her basis amount to determine how much can be distributed by the business to that owner tax-free.

EXAMPLE: Rafael and Ramona run Hamlets LLC, a pet boarding, grooming, and supply store for large-breed canines. They each began with a $10,000 basis in their LLC. (They paid in $10,000 each to start the business.) The LLC operating agreement allocates profits, losses, and capital interests equally to the two members. In their first year, net profits from the business equaled $75,000, allocated equally ($37,500) to each member.

This automatic allocation (pass-through) and taxation of profits is taxed to each owner at their individual income tax rates. This allocation also increases each partner's basis in their interest, so each has a basis in their interest at the end of the first year of $47,500. The owners have a provision in their LLC operating agreement that says the members will be distributed 40% of any net profits allocated to each member within three and one-half months of the close of the tax year. This guarantees that the owners will have cash on hand to pay taxes owed on allocated LLC profits when they file their prior year individual income tax returns on April 15 of the following year. (In fact, the owners should have estimated and paid these taxes throughout the year in quarterly installments.) This means that the LLC will write each owner a check for $15,000 ($37,500 × 40% = $15,000) by April 15 of the second year.

This distribution of profits lowers the basis of each owner from $47,500 to $32,500. The owners are not taxed on the distribution in the second year because each has sufficient basis to "absorb" the amount of the distribution. The owners would get taxed only if the distribution exceeded the basis in their interest, and the tax would be applied only to the amount that exceeded their basis. For example, if the LLC had sufficient cash to pay out $60,000 to each member by April 15 of the second year, $47,500 of the payout would decrease each member's basis in his or her interest to zero, and the excess payout of $12,500 ($60,000 − $47,500 = $12,500) would be taxable income to each member in the second year.

The discussion about income tax basis, above, mentions partnerships and LLCs (and even S corporations) but not sole proprietorships. They are omitted because a sole proprietor does *not* get an income tax basis in his or her sole proprietorship interest. IRS regulations say that sole proprietorships are "disregarded as entities separate from their owners," which is IRS-speak for saying that sole proprietorships are regarded as tax extensions of their individual owners. Money earned by the sole proprietorship does not pass through anything; it simply is the owner's personal income, reported by the owner on the owner's income tax return. When the sole proprietorship sells the business, for tax purposes he or she simply sells the individual assets, each of which has its own income tax basis. So, for tax purposes, because a sole proprietor cannot sell a separate interest in the business, the sole proprietor does not need to track his or her basis in that interest.

Corporate Tax Treatment

Regular corporations (known as "C" corporations because they are subject to Subchapter C of Title 26 of the Internal Revenue Code) require two levels of tax reporting and payment. Here's how it works: First, the corporation pays income taxes on profits retained in the business. Second, owners who are paid salaries or dividends on corporate profits must pay individual income taxes on these payments.

Although this double layer of taxation may seem burdensome, many businesses prefer corporate taxation to pass-through tax treatment, because it can result in an overall tax savings for the corporation's owners.

With pass-through taxation, all business profits pass through the business and are reported (and taxed) each year on the individual owner's income tax returns, at the owner's individual tax rate. This is so even if the profits are left in the business and not paid to the owners. As you make more money in your business each year, these profits are added to any individual income already reported on your tax return (such as your spouse's income, wages you earn in a regular employee job or as an independent contractor, and any other income you earn outside of your incorporated business). All of this income is taxed at your marginal— that is, your top (or highest)—individual tax rate. Ouch!

The more money your pass-through business earns, the larger your tax bill at the end of the year, even if you never see these profits because you leave them in the business. Some taxpayers must dig into personal savings to pay the extra individual income taxes on this "phantom income."

> **EXAMPLE:** Henry and Harriet own and operate an unincorporated "urban cowboy" hair styling salon, The Double-H Hair Roundup. The good news is that each owner expects to net $50,000 of additional income by year-end. The bad news is that this extra money will be taxed to each owner at his or her marginal (top) income tax rate of 35%.

Because corporations are treated as tax entities separate from their owners, profits left in a corporation are taxable only to the corporation (not to the owners), at corporate income tax rates. And the corporation can deduct profits paid out to owners who work in the business, such as salaries paid to the shareholder-employees of a small corporation, to arrive at its taxable income. These salaries are taxable only to the shareholder/employee, at his or her individual income tax rate, not to the corporation.

Because of this legal and tax separation between the corporation and its owners, the owners of a corporation can split business income between themselves and their business to spread business profits out across the lower corporate and individual income tax brackets.

> **EXAMPLE:** If the Double-H from the previous example incorporated, the owners could retain some or all of their earnings in their corporation, where it would be taxed at initial corporate income tax rates of 15% and 25%. Because these rates are lower than the marginal individual income tax rates of the owners, the owners would face a lower overall tax burden.

C corporations may retain up to $250,000 of earnings without raising any eyebrows at the IRS (special types of personal service corporations are allowed a lesser automatic retained earnings amount of $150,000). C corporations can retain earnings higher than these amounts as long as the owners have a valid business purpose for keeping money in the corporation and are not simply sheltering earnings in the corporation to avoid payouts to shareholders. (Why avoid payouts? Because dividends paid to shareholders get taxed to each shareholder at dividend tax rates.)

Tax Treatment of Corporate Dividends

Federal tax law has lowered the income tax rate individuals must pay on corporate dividends to 15% (low-income taxpayers pay only 5%) through 2010. This money is taxed separately from other individual income, that is, dividends are not added to other personal income and taxed at the individual's marginal (top) tax rate. Previously, dividends were taxed, like other personal income, at the marginal (top) income tax rates of the owners, which typically are well above 15%.

A corporation cannot deduct dividends it pays out to shareholders from its taxable income. This means that dividends are taxed twice: once to the corporation as part of its taxable income, and once to the shareholder at the dividend tax rates described above. Proposals have popped up over the years to change the federal tax law to make dividends deductible by the corporation, and therefore subject to just one level of income tax at the individual shareholder level. No one knows whether this deductible-dividend proposal will ever make it out of a Congressional committee room.

Under long-standing federal tax law, corporations also get an income tax break on dividend income they earn as shareholders. Corporations that hold shares in other corporations may exclude 70% to 100% of dividend income from the corporation's taxable income. This is why it often makes sense for corporations to invest in the stock of other corporations.

Changing Your Tax Classification

Now that you know how money is taxed in each type of business entity, you're better prepared to choose a structure for your business. If you already have a business, you're in a better position to determine whether you should convert to another business form. (Chapters 6 through 9 discuss the most common conversion scenarios.)

But what if you are perfectly happy with your business entity, except for your tax treatment? Can you change only your tax classification— from pass-through to corporate (or vice versa)—without converting to a new business entity?

With some exceptions, the answer is yes! Most entities have the flexibility to change their default tax classification if the owners wish to do so. This principle, known as "Entity Classification Election" (or "special election"), allows a partnership to be taxed like a corporation or lets the owners of a corporation enjoy pass-through tax treatment.

This section explains the rules for these special tax entity elections.

> **TIP**
>
> **Don't change your tax status on a whim.** It's good to know that you may not be stuck with a default tax classification, especially if your business changes and you want to shop around for more advantageous tax treatment. However, it's usually best to pick a business entity whose default tax classification will work for you right out of the gate. Changing your tax classification will have some long-term consequences. For example, once you change the tax classification of your business, the IRS will require you to wait five years before changing its status again. Although there are some exceptions to this five-year rule, they might not apply to your situation. Before you decide to change the tax treatment of your business, consult your tax adviser.

Changing the Tax Classification of an Unincorporated Business

Unincorporated business entities such as LLCs (both single-owner and multiple-owner) and partnerships (both general and limited) can change from pass-through to corporate tax treatment. To do this, you must check the appropriate box on IRS Form 8832, *Entity Classification Election.* Once you file this form, your unincorporated business will be treated exactly like a corporation under the Internal Revenue Code for all purposes, including income tax reporting and paying, employee fringe benefits, stock option plans, and sale and redemptions of interests in the business.

Once the election is effective, the unincorporated business files corporate tax returns and may split business income between the business, which now pays corporate income taxes on retained profits, and the individual owners, who now pay individual income taxes on salaries paid out to them as "corporate" employees. Payments for services performed by the owners will be treated as corporate salaries, and the corporation may deduct them from its taxable income. Direct distribution of business profits to the owners will be treated and taxed as corporate dividends. Further, if an owner sells his or her interest in the unincorporated business in the future, the IRS will treat and tax that transaction as a sale of corporate stock.

EXAMPLE: Kitsch Kitchens, LLC, designs and installs custom-made kitchen cabinetry. The company is owned and operated by Karen and Karl, a married couple. Due to a recent boom in home remodeling and construction, profits are strong. Most of the extra money is put back into the business to buy inventory and make capital improvements. Karen and Karl don't want to pay taxes at their top individual income tax rates on these phantom earnings. They wonder whether they should incorporate their business so that retained business profits are taxed at lower 15% and 25% initial corporate income tax rates.

If Karen and Karl file IRS Form 8832 to elect corporate tax treatment, their business remains an LLC legally under state law but is taxed as a corporation under federal tax law (most states will also treat the business as a corporation for state income tax purposes once the federal election is made). The tax election allows them to split income between themselves and their LLC, spreading it among the lower corporate and individual income tax brackets (instead of having it all taxable at their top individual income tax rates). The money retained in the LLC is taxed at the lower 15% and 25% corporate income tax rates. The money paid out to Karl and Karla in return for working for their LLC is now treated as a "corporate" salary, which is deducted from the LLC's income and taxed only to Karen and Karl on their joint individual income tax return. Because they elected corporate tax status, Karen and Karl's total LLC and individual taxes on business earnings are less than they would have paid had all LLC earnings been taxed at their individual income tax rates.

Can Sole Proprietors Change Their Tax Treatment?

Can a sole proprietor make a corporate tax treatment election? This election appears to apply only to business "entities," and, technically, the sole proprietorship is not considered a business entity under the federal tax regime. As a result, a sole proprietor may not be able to file IRS Form 8832 to change its business tax classification. If you own a sole proprietorship and want to change its tax status, talk to you tax adviser to find out what your options are.

Changing the Tax Classification of a Corporation

Corporations can change their tax classification from corporate to pass-through treatment. However, corporations cannot directly adopt the pass-through tax treatment of a sole proprietorship or partnership. Instead, the Internal Revenue Code (and parallel provisions found in the tax law of most states) creates a special form of pass-through tax treatment for corporations under Subchapter S of Title 26 of the IRC, called the S corporation tax election. For more information on converting a C (regular) corporation to an S corporation, see Chapter 9.

Paying Out Profits

Deciding how you want to pay out profits is one of the more pleasant parts of picking the right business entity. There are legal, tax, and practical differences in how each entity pays out profits, and these differences are important to owners and investors. How profits are paid depends on the type of business and the type of owner.

Sole Proprietorships

All profits earned by a sole proprietor automatically end up in the owner's pockets and are taxed to the owner—a simple rule for a relatively simple form of business.

General Partnerships

In a partnership, things are a little different, because the business is a separate entity from the owners. This distinction between the business and the owners can cause what is known as "phantom income" to the partners. Phantom income is income that is taxed to a partner even though he or she does not receive it (a scary thought that deserves a scary title). Here's how it works: A partnership, like a sole proprietorship, is a pass-through tax entity, so all income earned in the business passes through the business and ends up on the individual tax returns of the partners. The difference between a partnership and a sole proprietorship, however, is that the partners may not actually receive the money, even though it is taxed to them. The partnership agreement determines whether income earned by the partnership actually gets paid out to the partners each year.

The idea of being taxed on money you don't receive is bad enough; what's even worse is that partners may have to dig into their personal savings or other income just to come up with the money they owe the government for "earning" this phantom income.

To avoid this result, partners often adopt a procedure to make sure that they receive at least enough money from the partnership to pay the taxes on automatically allocated phantom income. The procedure is usually accomplished by a provision in the partnership agreement known as a distributions clause, which requires profits to be distributed to the owners each year in an amount sufficient for them to pay the taxes each owes on the profits.

LLCs

As pass-through tax entities, co-owned LLCs must also deal with the phantom income issue that affects partnerships, as described above. Commonly, LLC owners address the issue with a distributions clause in their operating agreement, which provides for an annual payment to each owner that is sufficient to pay the taxes each owes on the profits. The provision usually includes a formula allowing each member to receive a percentage of his or her allocated profits equal to the highest federal and state tax rates combined:

Member's share of allocated profits × (highest federal income tax rate + highest state income tax rate) = annual distribution.

EXAMPLE: Jason is a 50% owner of an LLC that has $100,000 in net profits at the end of the tax year. Jason's share of net profits is $50,000. Assume the current highest individual tax rates at the federal and state level are 35% and 11%, respectively. If Jason's LLC operating agreement requires distributions according to the above formula, Jason will be distributed $23,000 (50,000 × 46%) at the end of the tax year so he can pay the IRS and state taxes on his allocated LLC net profits.

The equation above usually gives the LLC member more than enough cash to pay individual income tax on allocated net profits, for several reasons:

- Most people pay an overall income tax rate (called an "effective" income tax rate) that is less than their top ("marginal") maximum rate because of the way the "progressive" income tax brackets work. No matter how high their total income, all taxpayers pay a lower tax rate on the first dollars they earn, up to a threshold amount. Once they earn enough to jump to the next tax bracket, they pay tax on their additional income at this level, and so on. So, even though taxpayers might pay tax at the highest rate for some of the money they earn, their effective tax rate will be lower.

- Individuals can generally deduct any state income taxes they had to pay on their federal income tax return.

- Individuals may also use other deductions, personal exemptions, and credits to further reduce the tax they owe.

Corporations

In a corporation, profits are paid out primarily as salaries or dividends:

- **Salaries.** If an owner works for the corporation as an officer or employee—as most owners of small, closely held corporations do—the owner can receive payouts in the form of a salary. The salary is deducted from corporate income, because the IRS considers reasonable salary payments to be an ordinary and necessary business expense. Therefore, the salary is only reported as income and taxed once, on the individual income tax return of the corporate owner-employee.

- **Dividends.** Corporate owners also are investors in the stock of the corporation, and as stockholders they can receive payouts in the form of dividends. Both salaried and passive investors can receive dividends (but passive investors cannot receive a salary, because they don't work for the corporation). Because dividends cannot be deducted from corporate income, this money is taxed twice: once as income to the corporation, and again as income to the shareholder.

Because dividends are taxed twice, small, privately held corporations traditionally haven't paid out dividends to shareholders. Furthermore, many small corporations need to fund business growth with retained earnings rather than paying them out to investors. These corporations usually ask their investors to be patient and postpone any return on their investment until the corporation increases in value and creates a market for its shares.

When a Dividend Isn't Really a Dividend: Decoding Corporate E & P

Not every payment by a corporation to shareholders is considered a dividend. Under the Internal Revenue Code, a dividend means money paid out of "earnings and profits" (E & P) of the corporation. If a payment does not fit within this definition, it is considered, for tax purposes, to be a "return on capital" and is taxed at the capital gains tax rates.

Since the current dividends tax rates and long-term capital gains tax rates are 15% for most taxpayers, what's the difference? There are two:

- When a payout is treated as a return of capital, only the portion of the payout that exceeds the shareholder's basis in shares is taxed; the entire amount of a dividend is always taxed.

- The current 15% dividend tax rate is scheduled to end after 2010. Unless Congress extends the current dividends tax break, dividends after 2010 will be subject to tax at each shareholder's marginal ordinary income tax rate, which normally is higher than the capital gains tax rate that will apply.

In making the determination as to whether a payment is treated as a dividend or capital gains, the key factor is how the E & P is calculated. For IRS purposes, it must be calculated by making certain plus and minus adjustments to corporate net taxable income to arrive at the "real" money earned by the corporation.

For example, accelerated depreciation—which often is subtracted for tax purposes—is added back in when calculating E & P for tax purposes. Similarly, federal taxes paid, which are not deducted from taxable income, are subtracted from taxable income when calculating E & P, since they represent a real economic outlay made by the corporation.

There are a number of additional special rules to consider. For example, if your corporation makes a profit this year and calculates a positive E & P for this year, money paid out to investors this year will be treated as a dividend (known as a "nimble dividend") to the extent of this year's current E & P amount, even if your corporation has accumulated a negative E & P balance carried over from prior years. Below are examples of three scenarios that may arise when paying out profits to corporate shareholders.

When a Dividend Isn't Really a Dividend: Decoding Corporate E & P (cont'd)

EXAMPLE 1: Phil and Buster own a corporate commercial office cleaning franchise called Crud Busters, Inc. They are funded by a small investment group. The early years of operation were growth years, which lost money, but the current year is a profitable one with positive earnings and profits. The board decides to declare and issue a $50,000 total dividend to the shareholders. The payout will be treated and taxed to the shareholders as a dividend (at the current 15% preferential dividends tax rate to each owner), because the corporation has current year earnings and profits of $70,000.

EXAMPLE 2: Let's assume that in the early years, before Crud Busters, Inc., has positive E & P, the investors are clamoring for a payout, and the board agrees to make a distribution out of cash reserves. Fiona, an investor, gets $10,000 as her share of the distribution. It's not taxed to her as a dividend, since the payout did not come from positive earnings and profits. Instead, the payout reduces her basis in her shares. Let's assume Fiona's current basis in her shares is her original $15,000 cost basis—that is, the amount she originally paid for her shares. The $10,000 payout to Fiona simply reduces her basis to $5,000, and she pays no tax on the distribution.

EXAMPLE 3: Let's skip forward one more year and assume that Crud Busters, Inc. still has a negative E & P for the latest (as well as all previous) tax years. Let's also assume that the board decides to make another distribution out of cash reserves, and that Fiona gets another $10,000. This time, $5,000 of the payout reduces Fiona's basis in her shares to zero. The remaining $5,000 is taxed to Fiona at capital gains tax rates. If Fiona has held her shares for more than one year, she pays tax at the 15% long-term capital gains tax rate.

Start-Up Losses

In the start-up phase of a business, you may generate losses—that is, you may pay out more in business expenses than you earn in profits. Although you would probably prefer to start making money right from the get-go, a start-up loss is not always a major setback, particularly if you have other sources of income.

In an entity with pass-though status, such as an LLC, sole proprietorship, or partnership, business losses are not taxed at the entity level. Instead, subject to special rules and limits, losses pass through the business and are allocated to the owners each year. If owners of these business entities incur losses, they may be able to use them to offset earnings or investment income from other sources, such as a regular salaried day job or investment income from a stock or mutual fund portfolio.

Because of this pass-through tax treatment, some investors in the start-up phase of a business may prefer to invest in an LLC rather than a corporation. With an LLC, investors get both limited liability protection and the possibility of being able to use start-up business losses to offset other income reported on their individual income tax returns.

In a corporation, however, business losses are locked into the corporation. Even though they may be carried back and forward (within limits) to offset corporate income in earlier or later tax years, they generally cannot be used by the shareholders to offset income on their individual income tax returns.

The S corporation creates an exception to this rule. If a corporation makes an S corporation election, subject to special rules and limits, business losses (and profits) pass through the corporation and are reported on the individual income tax returns of the corporate shareholders. In other words, S corporation shareholders can often use S corporation losses to reduce their individual taxable income. Of course, an LLC obtains the same pass-through tax treatment with greater flexibility and fewer restrictions, so it usually makes more sense to form an LLC than to create an S corporation to pass losses through to the owners.

> **TIP**
>
> **Consider forming an LLC if you plan to take on business debts.** In an LLC, business debts, such as a mortgage the LLC takes out on real estate it owns, generally increase the income tax "basis" of the owners' LLC interest. An increased basis can help the owners reduce income taxes when they receive distributions of profits from the LLC. Distributions paid out by LLCs and partnerships are taxable to the owners only if (and to the extent that) they exceed the owners' income tax basis in their interest in the business. Investors in an S corporation do not receive a stepped-up basis when the company takes on debt (unless the shareholders directly and personally lend the money to the corporation), so this advantage is not available to them.

Institutional and Venture Capital

A corporation may be the best business entity to form if you want to cast a wider net for investment capital. Institutional investors and lenders and venture capitalists generally prefer to fund corporations because they are accustomed to the way standard corporate paperwork and instruments define and protect their interests.

For example, a corporation's articles can authorize classes of preferred shares that give certain investors special rights to dividends and liquidation assets. Preferred shares can also come with special voting rights. For example, a corporation could issue a class of preferred shares to a venture capital fund, allowing it to separately elect one or two people to the corporation's board of directors. A corporation can also issue preferred stock that can be converted—at the option of the stockholder—into a greater number of common shares of the corporation.

Once a venture firm becomes comfortable with the organization and performance of the corporation, it can convert its preferred shares into a greater number of common shares to increase its investment in the firm—and give up its preferred stock rights to dividends or liquidation assets that it no longer feels are necessary to ensure a return on its investment.

Stock options and warrants (which are stock options issued to an investor or lender to buy stock at a fixed price) are other standard corporate instruments sought by private capital sources seeking to invest in a promising business. Corporate stock options and warrants represent a binding promise from the corporation to sell the investor or lender additional shares at a fixed price. If the corporation uses the initial funds paid in or loaned by the capital firm wisely, the value of the corporation's shares will increase, and the investor can "capitalize" on this success by buying additional shares at the negotiated option or warrant price, which will be lower than the fair market value of the appreciated shares.

With a bit of work (and significant legal fees), it would be possible to custom-tailor an LLC operating agreement to accomplish many of the same results achieved by the corporate instruments mentioned above, but generally this is too much of a bother. Besides, capital fund managers prefer relying on tried-and-true tax strategies specifically provided to corporations under the Internal Revenue Code rather than testing the tax waters with newly invented strategies custom-tailored to an LLC.

Many corporate tax provisions provide a direct benefit to the founders of small businesses, too. For example, the Internal Revenue Code contains corporate stock redemption provisions that allow owners to sell their shares back to their corporation and have the transaction treated as an "exchange" rather than as a payout of profits to the owners (in other words, rather than as a dividend). This means that the owners pay capital gains tax rates, not dividend tax rates, on the exchange. Although the capital gains tax rate is currently the same as the tax rate on dividends (15% for most taxpayers), there still is a big benefit for this "exchange" treatment: An owner who redeems stock in a qualified exchange pays tax only on the amount that exceeds his or her income tax basis in the shares. If the stock redemption were treated as a dividend payout rather than an exchange, the entire sales price would be taxed.

Capital gains tax treatment (and dividend tax treatment under the newer federal rules) is a tax advantage of setting up a corporation. Your interest in your business is represented by shares of stock, which you or your heirs can later sell, paying only capital gains tax rates (or sometimes dividend tax rates). For most taxpayers and most transactions, these rates are currently set at 15%. In an unincorporated business, profits are pulled out of the business each year and pass through to the owners, who must pay tax on these profits at their marginal (top) individual income tax rates, which can go as high as 35%.

Planning for a Public Offering

Corporations have the edge over all other types of business entities when it comes to selling ownership interests to the public. In fact, the securities industry and its laws are specifically designed for the public acquisition of corporate shares.

For example, established commercial and securities laws govern the offering, sale, and transfer of shares of stock. And most public stockholders know that they will share proportionately in the dividends and value of the corporation they invest in. This is the essence of a stockholder's interest in a corporation.

The same is not true of an investment in an LLC or any other noncorporate business entity, because the nature and marketability of a business interest in these entities is less certain. LLCs and partnership have the flexibility to split profits, losses, voting power, and liquidation proceeds in disproportionate ways, and an investor must carefully examine the company's formal business documents to understand the rights and restrictions associated with investing in the company.

Another reason why corporations are such effective vehicles for public offerings is that corporations, unlike pass-through entities, do not automatically allocate earnings and profits to investors. Instead, corporation profits are only allocated (and taxed) to shareholders when the board of directors declares a dividend. And dividends, unlike the profits of an unincorporated business, must be paid out to shareholders once they are allocated (declared) by the board. In other words, a corporate shareholder pays tax on real income he or she actually receives, not on phantom income that may stay in the business bank account.

This does not mean that you should rule out forming an unincorporated business entity if you are planning to grow a big business. For example, LLCs often work best as an entity of choice at the early or middle stages of business growth. And you can usually convert an LLC to a corporation without harsh tax consequences when the time is right. In fact, an LLC is often the best entity to form when you're starting or building up a business, before you're ready to incorporate and seek out venture capital funding.

> **CAUTION**
>
> **Publicly traded interests in a limited partnership are subject to special restrictions.** For a brief period, crafty underwriting firms (companies that sell initial shares of a company to the public markets) and their lawyers succeeded in selling limited partnership interests on public trading markets. However, this tactic has essentially been shut down by the IRS, which enacted "publicly traded partnership" rules that treat these LPs as corporations for income tax purposes. Before these rules were devised, the LPs were selling their interests to the public but hanging on to pass-through taxation for their business, to avoid the double tax that applies to payouts of corporate dividends. In effect, promoters of publicly traded LP interests tried to do an end run around the double-tax corporate tax regime. The IRS rules put a stop to this by imposing corporate tax rules on LPs that act like corporations by selling ownership interests to the public.

S Corporations and Public Investment Don't Mix

S corporations, unlike regular (C) corporations, are not the right choice for businesses that seek public investment. S corporations may have no more than 100 shareholders, who generally must be individuals (not corporations or other business entities) who are U.S. citizens. These restrictions mean that S corporation shares can't be freely sold to public markets.

Clever tax advisers have worked the rules and found ways around them—for example, forming several S corporations, each of which has 100 shareholders and runs a division of a larger enterprise—but these tricks should be left to the experts (who will charge you a bundle to implement this sort of strategy and defend it if the IRS audits your business tax returns).

Another impediment to using an S corporation to attract capital is that it can have only one class of stock; different classes of shares that allow preferences to certain shareholders are not allowed. And even though proposals have been advanced to change the Internal Revenue Code to increase the number of permitted shareholders and to liberalize or eliminate other S corporation restrictions, the practical reality is that any limitation on the number or type of shareholders or shares will prevent the S corporation from being seen as an attractive investment by the public at large and by public underwriting firms.

Investors are also not too keen on investing in a pass-through entity like the S corporation. S corporation profits are allocated and taxed to shareholders each year, even if the profits are not paid out to the investors. Public investors generally do not want to be taxed on income earned by a business they invest in unless the income is actually paid out to them. (Paying taxes is painful enough, but no one likes to pay taxes on phantom income they never receive.)

Doing Business Out of State

Doing Business Out of State

Your decision to choose an LLC or corporation may be affected by your ability to do business out of state. Crossing a state line to transact business can have a profound impact on your company. It can affect whether you must register as a foreign (out-of-state) company, how much state income and sales tax you must pay or collect, and where your company must travel to defend a lawsuit.

If you disregard your company's out-of-state obligations, you may be fined or face other legal sanctions. For example, a defendant whom you sue in another state can ask a court to delay or dismiss your lawsuit until you qualify your corporation or limited liability company (LLC) in that state and pay any late-qualification fees and late filing penalties you owe (which can be substantial).

Some of these out-of-state responsibilities—such as preparing registration paperwork, paying a qualification fee, and appointing an agent in another state—may seem bothersome. After all, you probably had enough of that sort of work when you formed your corporation or limited liability company. But as your company expands outside of its state of organization, you must deal with the bureaucracy that follows.

When it comes to doing business out of state, the rules regarding LLCs and corporations are similar. To that extent, this may not figure in your decision whether to operate as an LLC or corporation. Nonetheless, it's a good idea to familiarize yourself with the rules in this chapter before proceeding as either entity. The information will be especially useful for corporations and limited liability companies that:

- organize in one state but have their principal location in another state
- organize in one state but are located near the borders of other states in which they transact business or sell goods or services
- organize in one state but plan to expand nationally (or regionally) to sell products or services, or

• do most or a significant part of their business over the Internet, by mail, or by phone.

Domestic Versus Foreign

Your company is a domestic corporation or a domestic LLC in your state of organization. The term "state of organization" refers to the state where you incorporate your corporation or form your LLC. In every other state, your company is considered a foreign corporation or foreign LLC. Foreign simply means out of state, not out of the United States.

What Does "Doing Business" in Another State Mean?

The answer to "What is doing business in another state?" depends on why you are asking the question. If you want to know whether you must register your corporation or LLC in another state and pay or collect state taxes on transactions connected to the state or its residents, you will need to check the corporations, LLC, and tax laws or codes. We summarize these laws later in this chapter. These laws set standards for determining when a foreign company's activities are significant enough in the state to impose obligations on the out-of-state company.

On the other hand, if you are asking the question because you want to know whether you can be sued in another state (in other words, whether you must appear to defend your company in a lawsuit in another state), your degree of doing business is measured by standards contained in the state's long-arm statute. These laws establish when the state can reach out beyond its borders and get jurisdiction over your company for your activities and transactions within the state. (We summarize these rules below.)

Are the Rules for Doing Business Out of State the Same for Corporations and LLCs?

The rules for doing business out of state covered in this text are, for the most part, similar for corporations and limited liability companies. Any differences are small and usually have to do with administrative matters, such as the fee you must pay to qualify to do business in the state.

> **TIP**
>
> **The term "company" refers to both corporations and LLCs.** Because the rules about doing business out of state are similar for corporations and LLCs, the word "companies" in this text refers to both types of business entities. You will need to check the law in the state where you are doing business to find the specific requirements for your particular state and type of business entity.

What Are the Rules for Qualifying in Another State?

Your company must qualify to do business in any state where it is doing intrastate business. This usually means any state where your company has a physical presence or repeated business transactions *within* the state. There are some exceptions to this general rule. For example, if the only business your company is engaged in within a state is via mail order or telephone sales, you normally don't need to qualify to do business in that state. (The meaning of "intrastate business" and the rules about qualifying are discussed in more detail below.)

When Do You Have to Pay Income Tax or Collect Sales Tax in Another State?

An out-of-state company or its owners must pay state income tax if it earns income within a state (and that state imposes income taxes). The definition of income earned within a state can be complicated. Most states apportion income earned within and outside the state by using property, payroll, and sales factors. In addition to income tax, most states collect sales tax on the sale of tangible property (consumer products). Typically, sales tax will be imposed in a state if tangible personal property is sold and shipped from a physical location within the state, such as a warehouse or store.

Can Your Company Be Sued in Another State?

If your company has qualified to do business in another state (or if a court believes your company *should* have so qualified), you can be sued and forced to defend your company in that state. If your company does not have to qualify to do business in a state, then you will only have to defend a lawsuit there if your activities within the state bring you within the state's long-arm statute and you have sufficient contacts with the state so that a claim of jurisdiction over your company does not violate the U.S. Constitution.

Generally, an out-of-state company will fall within the reach of another state's jurisdiction if the company has a physical presence in the state, generates sufficient sales from its residents, advertises regularly in the state, or uses that state's facilities. (See below for more on personal jurisdiction.)

What About Business Done on the Internet?

Doing business on the Internet is less likely, by itself, to trigger corporate or LLC registration requirements or income or sales tax obligations. Doing business over the Internet, however, may be enough to require you to defend a lawsuit in another state, particularly if it relates to problems arising from your Internet sales. Even this, however, will depend in part on the type of transaction involved, the revenue derived from business within that state, and the impact of your business dealings. (See below for more on doing business in another state via the Internet.)

Qualifying to Do Business

To qualify your company to do business in another state, you must file paperwork, pay fees, appoint an agent in the foreign state, and abide by other rules and regulations. You may wonder why you must wade through so much red tape when you do business from state to state. After all, don't business and government leaders praise our supposedly borderless economy? Why must a business go through paperwork and be subject to new rules and regulations every time it crosses a state border?

There are legitimate reasons for states to regulate business conducted within their borders. Companies doing business in another state benefit from the foreign state's residents, services, and commerce. In return, it's fair to make these companies accountable to residents in their state courts. In addition, these rules allow states to make out-of-staters abide by the same corporate rules as locals. And finally—though not least important—the state can make money this way. When a business qualifies in a state, it pays a fee and also becomes visible to the state's tax agency, which collects state income, sales, and other taxes.

When Must You Qualify to Do Business in Another State?

Your company must qualify to do business in any state where it is engaged in *intrastate* business. This means that at least part of your business is conducted entirely within another state's borders. For example, if your business has a warehouse in another state and you sell and ship from the warehouse to customers within that state, you are engaged in intrastate business in that state.

On the other hand, a state can't make you qualify or pay taxes if you engage only in *interstate* business with that state—meaning all of your business is conducted across state lines. For example, if you sell and ship merchandise from your home state to residents in other states, you are engaged in interstate business, which cannot be regulated by the foreign state. Although every state has different variations on when a business must qualify as a foreign corporation or LLC, they all follow this same basic principle—companies must qualify if they are engaged in *intrastate* business that is not merely incidental to a larger *interstate* business operation.

Generally, if you have a physical presence in a state or repeated and successive business transactions within the state that are not interstate business, you are engaged in intrastate business and will be required to qualify. For example, if you pay employees located in another a state or rent or own real property in another state, you are more likely than not transacting business there and required to qualify.

You can also have intrastate business based on the services you render within a state. In one case, a national advertising agency made ads and bought airtime on Alabama television stations for an Alabama auto dealership. Even though the advertising company had no physical presence in Alabama (other than an employee who visited there occasionally), the ad agency's business was considered intrastate because "the primary purpose of the contract was the service of broadcasting the advertisements in the local area." (*Competitive Edge, Inc. v. Tony Moore Buick-GMC, Inc.* 490 So.2d 1242, 1246 (Ala. Ct. App. 1986).)

Whether a company is engaged in intrastate commerce is determined on a case-by-case basis. In making this determination, the following activities are often found to trigger qualification:

- **Sales of goods or services within a state.** If you sell goods from a location within a state—that is, the sale does not require approval from representatives of the company outside that state—or if the sale is made from inventory held in that state, most states will require you to qualify there.

- **Providing services or labor.** Most states require qualification if your company provides services or labor within the state, unless the services or labor are incidental to an interstate sale.

• **Construction activity.** Construction companies operating in another state are usually required to qualify in the state because they are often located there for several months and maintain offices and employees there as well.

Sample Qualification Statute

Most states have adopted the Model Business Corporation Act for corporations and follow similar rules for LLCs. As a result, state rules for out-of-state companies transacting business are often very similar.

The California statute is set forth below. These rules are very similar to the rules adopted by other states.

Section 191 of the California Corporations Code

191. (a) For the purposes of Chapter 21 [which says that a corporation that transacts intrastate business must qualify with the state] "transact intrastate business" means entering into repeated and successive transactions of its business in this state, other than interstate or foreign commerce.

(b) A foreign corporation shall not be considered to be transacting intrastate business merely because its subsidiary transacts intrastate business.

(c) Without excluding other activities which may not constitute transacting intrastate business, a foreign corporation shall not be considered to be transacting intrastate business within the meaning of subdivision (a) solely by reason of carrying on in this state one or more of the following activities:

(1) Maintaining or defending any action or suit or any administrative or arbitration proceeding, or effecting the settlement thereof or the settlement of claims or disputes.

(2) Holding meetings of its board or shareholders or carrying on other activities concerning its internal affairs.

(3) Maintaining bank accounts.

> ### Sample Qualification Statute (cont'd)
>
> (4) Maintaining offices or agencies for the transfer, exchange, and registration of its securities or depositories with relation to its securities.
>
> (5) Effecting sales through independent contractors.
>
> (6) Soliciting or procuring orders, whether by mail or through employees or agents or otherwise, where such orders require acceptance without this state before becoming binding contracts.
>
> (7) Creating evidences of debt or mortgages, liens, or security interests on real or personal property.
>
> (8) Conducting an isolated transaction completed within a period of 180 days and not in the course of a number of repeated transactions of like nature.

CAUTION

Even though the rules for qualification are similar in many states, the exact requirements can differ from state to state. If you are in doubt about whether you should qualify in a state, check the state's laws and, if you still have questions, ask a lawyer.

What Activities Are *Not* Considered Intrastate?

States exempt certain types of business contacts from their definition of intrastate business. Some examples of the types of business activities that foreign corporations and LLCs can conduct without having to qualify are:

- appearing in court on behalf of your company, having settlement meetings, or mediating or arbitrating a dispute

- holding meetings of the board of directors or LLC managers, or carrying on other activities concerning the business's internal affairs

- maintaining bank accounts or securing or collecting debts, or enforcing a mortgage or security interest in property securing a debt

- selling through independent contractors

- soliciting or obtaining orders, whether by mail or through employees or agents or otherwise, if the orders require acceptance outside this state before they can become a contract, and

- engaging in an isolated transaction (often considered to be a business transaction) completed within 30 days and not part of a course of similar repeated transactions.

Some state statutes (Indiana and Florida, for example) specifically state that simply owning property or having a physical presence in the state is not enough, by itself, to require qualification. As a practical matter, however, once you buy property or rent office space in another state, chances are good that you will be conducting intrastate business in that state.

Other activities, not specifically mentioned in the Model Acts (see "Sample Qualification Statute," above), are also often not considered "doing business" for purposes of qualification. Some of these include national (not local) advertising campaigns, purchasing goods within the state at regular intervals, and certain installations and services incidental to interstate sales. In addition, if the only business your company is engaged in within a state is mail order or telephone sales, you normally don't need to qualify to do business in that state.

How Do You Qualify to Do Business in Another State?

Qualification is simply a registration process that involves filing paperwork and paying fees—similar to the procedures and fees required for incorporating. You must also designate a registered agent: a resident person or company in the state who agrees to accept legal papers on your behalf in the state. The qualification fees range from $100 to $300 (depending on the state).

The rules differ from state to state, but usually you must:

- Complete and file a Certificate of Authority (or similarly titled document) to transact business in the state. The certificate contains general information about your corporation or LLC, such as its name and address and a certification that it is in good standing in its state of formation.

- Publish a notice in a newspaper. If a state requires publication of a notice in a newspaper when a corporation or LLC is formed, it usually requires the same when a foreign corporation or LLC qualifies in the state. Local newspapers or corporate service providers can help you make this publication for a moderate fee.

- Pay your annual report fees (typically $50 to $100). These fees are due each year with the annual statement that gives the names of your directors and officers, your agent for service of process, and other basic information.

- Appoint a registered agent or registered agent business who will receive corporate documentation and accept service of process within the state. The registered agent may be a person who resides in the state and maintains an office there or a registered agent company that was formed or qualified to do business in the state and has an office there.

CAUTION

Annual fees in some states are high. Illinois and Massachusetts have high (multi-hundred-dollar) annual renewal fees. Although these states are the exception, not the rule, you should check state fees before engaging in activities that require qualification.

What Other Obligations Do You Incur After Qualifying?

Once you are registered in a state, the state revenue or tax agency will send you annual state income tax returns. You will have to report and pay state income and sales tax, as well as abide by state employment tax filings, if you have sufficient payroll, property, and sales in the state.

In some states, there is a minimum corporate income tax that companies must pay each year. In most states, the minimum tax is less than $100—although it can be significantly higher, such as in California or Massachusetts. California charges corporations and LLCs a minimum of $800 per year. California LLCs with gross receipts (which can include the cost of goods) of $250,000 or more pay significant additional annual fees ($900 to $11,000 or more per year).

If your company's name is similar to the name of a corporation or LLC already on file with the secretary of state, the state will ask you to add words to your name to make it different from the name of the existing corporation or LLC. The state's list can include the names of existing corporations and LLCs formed in the state as well as out-of-state corporations and LLCs already qualified in the state.

The state may also ask you to add an identifier to your corporate or LLC name if one is required under the state's corporate or LLC statutes. For example, many states require corporations formed in the state to include the word "Incorporated" or "Corporation" or a similar corporate designator (or an abbreviation of one of these words) in their name. Similarly, LLC statutes often require LLCs to include "Limited Liability Company" or an abbreviation of these words in their name. When the state asks you to choose an alternate name or add words to your existing name, this new name is known as your assumed or fictitious corporate or LLC name, and you will be required to do business in the state under this alternate name.

What About Branch Offices in Other States?

If you form your LLC or incorporate in one state and have branch offices in other states, you will probably have the full range of out-of-state responsibilities for each state in which you maintain a branch—provided that office does substantial business activities within the state and is engaged in intrastate business. For each state where you have that kind of presence, you will have to qualify to do business and collect and pay state income and sales taxes, and you will be subject to suit for your operations in that state.

Most state corporate and LLC statutes, however, exempt from qualification certain types of activities often engaged in by branch offices established for a limited purpose. States usually don't require a company to qualify if the only activities engaged in by a branch office are:

- maintaining the office or agency for the transfer, exchange, and registration of the company's own securities or depositaries

- making sales through independent contractors

- soliciting or procuring orders (whether by mail or through employees or agents or otherwise) where the orders must be accepted outside the foreign state to be finalized, or

- holding meetings of the company's board of directors or shareholders, or carrying on other activities concerning the company's internal affairs.

For example, if you set up an out-of-state branch office exclusively to let independent contractors call customers to make sales in the state, you may not need to qualify your company in that state. Be careful when claiming these exemptions, however, because state regulators may not always agree with your interpretation.

What Happens If You Fail to Qualify for Business?

If you fail to qualify, you can be subject to financial penalties known as late-qualification penalties. Under California law, for example, there is a late-qualification penalty of $250 plus $20 per day for willful (a knowing, not inadvertent) failure to qualify. These penalties can add up: If the California secretary of state determined that you willfully did business in California for two years prior to qualifying, the secretary of state could bill your company for approximately $15,000 ($365 × $20 × 2 years = $14,600 + $250 = $14,850).

Other states simply authorize the assessment of a flat amount for failure to qualify. These flat fees can range from the multi-hundred- to multi-thousand-dollar range.

Most states will also prevent companies that fail to qualify from bringing a lawsuit in that state's courts. Under these laws (known as closed-door statutes), a court will delay or dismiss your lawsuit if the defendant objects because you did not qualify your business in the state. In some states, your lawsuit will be dismissed; in others, it will be delayed until your company qualifies or pays any late-qualifications fees owed.

EXAMPLE: A developer, incorporated and located in Pennsylvania, purchased land in Vermont to build and sell condominiums. The developer entered into a contract with a Vermont supplier to purchase modular condominium units. When a dispute arose over the contract, the developer sued the supplier in Vermont. A court looked at the developer's activities in Vermont and determined that its ownership and use of the property in Vermont demonstrated that the developer should have qualified to do business there. The developer was, therefore, barred from suing the supplier in Vermont. (*Pennconn Enterprises, Ltd. v. Huntington*, 538 A.2d 673 (1987).)

If your case is dismissed, you may be able to refile your lawsuit as long as the time period for filing (known as the statute of limitations) has not expired. You will first have to qualify your business in the state and pay any late-qualification penalties you owe. If you don't want to qualify your business in the foreign state, you can file the same lawsuit in your state of organization, but you may run into a different problem: obtaining personal jurisdiction over the other company. (For more information on long-arm statutes and jurisdiction, see below.)

Remember, not every company that transacts business in a state must qualify to do business there. The standards vary and usually require repeated business dealings, often tied to a physical presence in a state. If your business in a state is primarily interstate commerce (for example, telephone, mail, or Internet sales with customers in the state), you probably don't need to worry about qualifying your business there, and the rules about delay and dismissal of lawsuits will not apply.

> **EXAMPLE:** A Canadian company entered into a contract in Vermont and engaged in some intrastate commerce in the state. When the company sued a customer in Vermont, the customer claimed that the suit was barred because the Canadian company failed to qualify in Vermont. The Vermont court held that the Canadian company's intrastate business activities in Vermont were incidental to an interstate purpose—and that the company's orders were taken primarily over the telephone. In short, the company did not have to qualify and was allowed to use the Vermont courts to sue the customer. (*Meunerie Sawyerville, Inc. v. Birt*, 637 A.2d 1082 (1994).)

Even if you failed to qualify when you should have, you are always entitled to defend yourself in a lawsuit in another state, and your contracts are always enforceable in that state. Some states make a point of stating these basic principles of law in their corporate or LLC statutes.

EXAMPLE: Section 808 of the New York Limited Liability Company Law states: *(b) The failure of a foreign limited liability company that is doing business in this state to comply with the provisions of this chapter does not impair the validity of any contract or act of the foreign limited liability company or prevent the foreign limited liability company from defending any action or special proceeding in any court of this state.*

Suing and Being Sued: Two Different Standards

The ability to sue someone in another state is different from the ability of an out-of-state company to force you into court in another state. In addition to the obvious difference—in one case you're bringing the lawsuit as a plaintiff, in the other you are the target of the lawsuit as a defendant—the standards used for each are different.

In general, a state can prevent you from using their courts to bring a lawsuit if you engage in intrastate business and fail to qualify—a standard that probably applies to a small fraction of companies. And you cannot be sued in a state if you can demonstrate that the state doesn't have jurisdiction over you under the state's long-arm statute.

In all cases, it makes sense to take a close look (or have an experienced lawyer or corporation service company take a close look for you) at the corporate and LLC statutes of the states in which you are engaged in more than an incidental amount of intrastate business. Read the definition of what qualifies as doing intrastate business in each state. If you conclude that your activities might be considered intrastate business, it's best to qualify to do business in those states. That way you know you can use that state's courts to enforce your contracts, and you will not have to pay a late-qualification fee. Better to deal with the inconvenience and modest filing fees ahead of time rather than face the higher fees, penalties, and delays in getting into court that you might otherwise face.

When Can You Use Your Trademarks in Another State?

A trademark is any distinguishing word, phrase, logo, or other signifier that identifies your goods (Coca-Cola or Nike, for example). A service mark does the same for services (FedEx or America Online, for example). For purposes of this guide, the term "trademark" is used to indicate both trademarks and service marks.

When your company qualifies to do business in another state, the secretary of state reviews and approves your corporate name for use in that state. This name approval process has no impact on your trademark rights—that is, getting clearance to use your corporate or LLC name in a state does not clear the way for you to use a trademark or to stop others from using similar trademarks. To guarantee your right to use a trademark in another state, you must perform a national trademark search. The search report will alert you to other uses of the identical or similar trademarks on similar goods or services. The Company Corporation (www.corporate.com) can assist you with a trademark search.

All states have laws under which trademarks may be registered and receive legal protection. However, there is not much practical benefit to registering your trademark in more than one state. Once you cross state lines with your products or services, you are engaged in interstate commerce and you can seek a federal registration for your trademark— a far more valuable form of trademark protection. Federal registration gives you national priority over competitors, allowing you to expand your protection as you move into new markets. State trademark protection, on the other hand, ends at each state's borders. In addition, federal registration gives your company a wider choice of remedies and places to file lawsuits.

State registration does have occasional benefits. If, for example, you operate almost exclusively within one state and do not plan to expand, you may find it less expensive and more practical to acquire a state trademark registration. Generally, however, federal registration is a one-stop source of protection that is superior to that offered by each state.

Paying and Collecting Taxes in Other States

When you do business outside of your state of formation, you may owe taxes to the foreign state where you are doing business. These taxes may include corporate income tax, personal income tax, employee withholding tax, employment taxes, and sales taxes. Your company's obligation to pay these taxes depends on various factors—all of which are ultimately tied to your intrastate activities (your business activities that occur solely within that state).

States use different standards and procedures to measure and impose these state taxes. Below, we look at some of the most common state taxes and how they are imposed.

When Do You Have to Pay Income Taxes to Another State?

Corporations and LLCs are treated differently under the tax laws, so we will discuss the two types of business entities separately.

C Corporations Versus S Corporations

There are two types of corporations for tax purposes: a C corporation (also known as a regular corporation) and an S corporation. C corporations are separate taxpaying entities, whereas an S corporation is similar to an LLC—it is a pass-through entity and the owners, not the corporation, pay tax on corporate profits.

Corporations

A corporation (a C corporation) must pay state corporate income tax on the profits the company earns in each state. This tax is imposed by most states; Nevada, South Dakota, and Wyoming are exceptions. The fact that you incorporated or qualified to do business in a state does not always mean that you will have to pay corporate income tax to that state—your obligation to pay state income taxes normally depends on whether or not you earn money in that state.

As a practical matter, most corporations owe state corporate income tax in their state of incorporation and in every state where they are qualified to do business. These are the states where they are most likely to earn their money, and they are also under the scrutiny of the state tax agency. So, if you plan to go into another state to make or set up sales operations (other than phone or Internet sales), hire and pay employees, or own property—expect to pay state corporate income tax there and to have to file out-of-state annual state corporate income tax returns.

How much tax must you pay to each state? Because it would be unfair for each state to tax *all* of a multistate company's profits, state laws usually apportion the profits based on a company's payroll, property, and sales in the state. Small, privately held corporations usually earn most or all of their income in their home state and have most of their business and property there as well, so that is where they typically have to pay the most state corporate income tax.

Harmonizing the Rules for Out-of-State Business Taxation

The Uniform Division of Income for Tax Purposes Act (UDITPA) has been adopted or is followed in many states. It apportions the income of corporations and other businesses for tax purposes according to property, sales, and payroll factors. For more information on the UDITPA, go to the Multistate Tax Commission website, at www.mtc.gov.

Limited Liability Companies

LLCs (like partnerships and S corporations) do not normally pay income taxes. Instead, the LLC's income flows through to the owners of the LLC, who declare and pay tax on their allocated profits on their individual federal and state income tax returns. This is true even though these profits are often not actually paid to the LLC owners.

Flow-Through Tax Treatment

LLCs and S corporations are pass-through tax entities—that is, the LLC's or S corporation's profits pass through to the owners at the end of each year. The owners are taxed on these profits at the owner's individual income tax rates.

CAUTION

Taxes on LLC profits and wages are treated separately. The payment of individual income tax on an LLC's allocated profits is separate from the LLC's payment of state income tax on wages paid to employees. We discuss the employee tax question below.

If the LLC owner resides in one state and the LLC income is earned in another state, which state can impose personal income tax on the LLC profits? Usually, both states can. To avoid double taxation, you may have to pay an income tax on LLC profits to one state and receive a tax credit in your home state. For example, many states require qualifying LLCs to withhold state income tax from their profits. Subsequently, the home state of the owners provides a tax credit for out-of-state taxes already withheld on this income.

When Do You Have to Withhold State Personal Income Taxes?

If your corporation or LLC has employees who work primarily from an out-of-state location, your company will need to withhold out-of-state personal income tax from employee wages. This is true for all states except those that do not impose personal income tax, including Florida, Nevada, South Dakota, Texas, Washington, and Wyoming. If the employee performs services in more than one state, you will have to make these deductions based on the amount of time the employee works in each state.

If the employee is a resident of the state of organization, the company must first withhold the income tax required by the other (foreign) state's tax laws. If the amount withheld to satisfy the foreign state's requirements is less than the amount that would have been withheld if the income was earned in the state of organization, the corporation or LLC must withhold this additional amount as well and pay it to the state of organization.

EXAMPLE: Nancy is an employee of GetGo, a California corporation. She resides in California but works six months of the year in GetGo's New York office. GetGo must withhold and pay New York income tax for the six-month period she works in New York. If the California withholding amount required on her wages during that six-month period in New York exceeds the actual amount withheld for New York personal income tax, GetGo must withhold the difference and pay it to California (with the California personal income tax for the six-month period that Nancy works in California).

If Nancy works six months of the year in Texas, which does not impose a personal income tax, her entire annual salary is subject to California withholding.

When Do You Have to Withhold and Pay Other State Employment Taxes?

When your employees perform services in more than one state, you may also be responsible for state employment taxes in other states. These taxes consist of state unemployment, disability insurance, training, and other forms of employer/employee employment taxes.

When a state demands payment of these taxes, its claim is based primarily on the *employee's* connection to the state, not the company's. Each state uses a four-part test to determine whether it should seek employment taxes. The key issue is whether all or most of an employee's services are performed in the state, with only incidental services performed outside the state. When this happens, the employee's services are considered localized in the state and all wages paid to that employee are subject to the state's employment tax.

If the issue can't be determined using the localized test, the state will consider other factors, such as whether the employee provides some services in the state and uses the state as a base of operations, and whether the state is the place from which the company exercises basic direction and control over the employee's work. Finally, the employee's state of residence—that is, where the employee has a permanent living place—may factor into the decision.

If an employee's wages are subject to state employment tax in a state, the *entire* wages are subject to employment taxes in that state. State employment taxes are not apportioned based on the amount of wages earned in each state as is done for personal income taxes. In other words, all states have agreed that the state where the first test applies is the state that will impose and collect employment tax on all of an employee's wages paid by the company (even if only a portion of the employee's services are performed in the taxing state).

When Do You Have to Pay Sales Tax to Another State?

Businesses are required to collect sales tax on transactions in any state where the company has a sufficient physical presence (such as a store, warehouse, or employees). The degree of presence may vary, but when it is sufficient to justify sales tax, it is referred to as a nexus.

For example, if your business is located in Arizona and you sell mail order jackets to a customer in New York and have no physical presence there, you do not have a nexus with New York and do not have to collect and pay sales tax there. You also don't have to collect California sales tax from a California resident who purchases an item while visiting your company's store in Arizona—even if you have a physical presence in California—because there is no connection between the sale and your presence in California.

Sales Tax Versus Use Tax

Even if your business does not collect sales tax on a purchase, a consumer in a state that collects sales taxes owes the money (in theory) to his or her state in the form of a use tax.

Sales and use taxes are two sides of the same coin. If a sales tax on a particular item is not collected by the seller, the buyer is supposed to pay the tax directly to the state where he or she resides. Theoretically, use taxes are the state's backup plan to make sure that it collects revenue on every taxable item "used" within its borders.

Traditionally, states have only attempted to collect a use tax on big-ticket items that require a license, such as cars and boats. In part, this was because collecting use taxes on smaller purchases was too much trouble. Some states have stepped up their efforts to collect use taxes on other, unlicensed significant purchases. Nevertheless, because most state agency resources are limited, there is no genuine effort to make people pay this tax for small purchases.

Lawsuits in Other States

Consider this unpleasant scenario: Your company is incorporated and located in Michigan. A process server delivers a summons to your secretary. According to the summons, a company has filed a lawsuit in Alabama claiming that your company's product is defective. You have not qualified to do business in Alabama and have no physical presence there. Can you ignore the summons? Can you force the company to bring their case in Michigan?

The answers depend on whether the Alabama courts can claim personal jurisdiction over your business. Personal jurisdiction refers to the state's ability to bind you by its decision. Or, put another way, personal jurisdiction is what validates the service of process and makes the court's judgment enforceable throughout the United States. You can be forced to appear in Alabama (or risk a default judgment being entered against you if you choose not to appear) if your contacts with Alabama bring you within the reach of the state's long-arm statute and meet the constitutionally mandated minimum contacts requirement.

How Can You Fight Jurisdiction If You Can't Appear in the State?

A state will always acquire personal jurisdiction over anyone who consents to a lawsuit. Consent is usually shown by voluntarily appearing to defend the lawsuit—for example, you send a lawyer to file a response to the charges against your company. If your appearance in court indicates consent, how do you fight personal jurisdiction? Courts have a special appearance rule that allows your lawyer to show up and argue the limited issue of whether the court has jurisdiction over your company. If you lose the jurisdiction battle, any further appearances will constitute consent to the lawsuit.

When Can Your Company Be Forced to Defend Itself in Another State?

Unless you have qualified to do business in a foreign state, a court in that state cannot force your company to appear there for a lawsuit unless you fall within the reach of the state's long-arm jurisdiction. Each state's long-arm statute describes the circumstances or situations where the state's personal jurisdiction can be extended over out-of-state companies or individuals. Long-arm statutes differ—some list activities that provide a basis for jurisdiction, and some simply proclaim that the state has jurisdiction in any situation that does not violate the Constitution (giving the judges the freedom to assess activities).

The U.S. Supreme Court has also established a minimum contacts constitutional standard that must be met before a state can require an out-of-state company to appear in its state courts. Under this constitutional standard, a company must have sufficient minimum contacts with the state before the company can be forced to appear and defend itself in that state (referred to as the "forum state"). For out-of-state businesses, these contacts consist of sufficient sales, advertising, or a physical presence such as sales agents or offices.

The minimum-contacts standard applies in combination with the state long-arm statute provisions. For example, many long-arm statutes provide that the transaction of any business in the state establishes jurisdiction. This provision is subject to the minimum-contacts requirement. A company cannot be forced to travel to another state for a lawsuit unless the state can show that there were sufficient minimum contacts. Otherwise it would offend what the Supreme Court has called "traditional notions of fair play and substantial justice."

A Typical Long-Arm Statute (Michigan)

Michigan's long-arm statute provides for personal jurisdiction over anyone who engages in the following activities:

(1) The transaction of any business within the state.

(2) The doing or causing any act to be done, or consequences to occur, in the state resulting in an action for tort.

(3) The ownership, use, or possession of any real or tangible personal property situated within the state.

(4) Contracting to insure any person, property, or risk located within this state at the time of contracting.

(5) Entering into a contract for services to be performed or for materials to be furnished in the state by the defendant.

Mich. Comp. Laws § 600.715.

As a practical matter, states can usually establish personal jurisdiction over an out-of-state company that owns or possesses real property in the state, commits a tort that causes injury to a state resident, or transacts business in the state—provided the minimum-contacts requirement is met.

Your Company Owns or Possesses Real Property in the State

Owning or possessing real property is a common basis for establishing personal jurisdiction. After all, a company that owns or leases property within a state should be prepared to defend itself in that state's courts, particularly in regard to matters that arise from the property.

Your Company Commits a Tort in the State

Generally, courts require nonresidents who commit torts (a type of act that causes damage or injury) in another state to appear and defend themselves in the state. After all, it simply wouldn't be fair to allow a nonresident to throw a rock over a state border and then avoid personal jurisdiction. Common torts include defamation, invasion of privacy, battery, negligence, and product liability. For example, if your company dumps pollutants into a river that flows into a nearby state, you will have to defend the lawsuit in that other state because it is an intentional (or negligent) activity harming residents. This legal principle derives from a series of cases from the 1930s, when states first claimed jurisdiction over out-of-state motorists who entered the state, caused an accident, and left.

You Transact Business in the State

Even if you are not qualified to do business in another state, a judge can decide that your company's activities—usually measured by your business contacts with the forum state—meet state and constitutional requirements for establishing jurisdiction. When measuring the degree of business being transacted in the state, judges often consider the following factors:

- **Money earned within the state.** Courts will consider the amount of money your company earns from its business within the state, as well as what percentage of the company's total revenues are derived from business in the state. For example, a court will consider the fact that your company earns $100,000 from its state's residents, which accounts for one-fifth of the company's total revenue.

- **Physical presence in the state.** Courts will look at whether you own or rent real estate; maintain offices, warehouses, stores, and the like; or employ people within the state. If these factors are present, you are usually considered physically present in the state and subject to suit in that state.

> EXAMPLE 1: BadDog, a New York corporation with an office and store in New York, sells skateboards over the Internet. A Los Angeles resident sues BadDog in California over a defective skateboard. BadDog's

degree of doing business in California—one-fifth of its sales are to California residents—is sufficient to require it to defend the lawsuit there.

EXAMPLE 2: BadDog opens a store in San Francisco. Because it now maintains a physical presence and employs salespeople in California, BadDog is doing business to a degree that allows it to be sued in California, regardless of the amount of revenue it generates from its California sales.

The jurisdictional standards advanced by the Supreme Court—minimum contacts and fair play and substantial justice—have been the subject of debate for more than five decades. Some rules are clear, however, and a judge would probably conclude that minimum contacts exist in the following situations:

- A manufacturer maintains a branch office, store, or warehouse, or some other physical presence in the state in which the suit is filed.

- A merchant from another state sends mail order catalogs into the state in which the suit is filed.

- A ski lodge advertises extensively in the forum state.

- An insurance company employs salespeople who solicit business over the telephone in the state in which the suit is filed.

- An Internet service provider from another state does business with paid subscribers or takes online orders from customers in the state in which the case is filed.

Even though the term "minimum contacts" implies more than one contact, a single transaction can justify personal jurisdiction. In one case, a Texas insurance company sold a policy to a California resident—the only policy it sold in California—and collected the premiums. According to the U.S. Supreme Court, that was enough to establish personal jurisdiction over the company for a California lawsuit arising from that policy. (*McGee v. International Life Ins. Co.* 355 U.S. 220 (1957).) Most long-arm statutes also support jurisdiction based on a single act—for example, any activity or transaction—although it must still meet the minimum-contacts standard. In addition, when a court analyzes your contacts with a forum state, it can only consider the contacts your company had prior to the date the claim arose.

Jurisdiction rules are often difficult to apply in the real world, and you may disagree with a judge as to whether your contacts were sufficient to justify having to appear in that state to defend a lawsuit. Unfortunately, there isn't always a simple answer. Courts throughout the country often differ on how these rules about personal jurisdiction should apply. If you have questions about your situation or find yourself in court over a jurisdictional issue, you should get professional help from a lawyer.

What Can Your Company Be Sued for in Another State?

Your company can be sued for *anything* in *any* state. However, you only have to appear to defend your company in states that can establish personal jurisdiction over you.

You should expect to have to appear for any lawsuit that arises directly from your activities within a state. For example, if you lease property and a dispute arises over the lease, the state will be able to obtain personal jurisdiction over you. Similarly, if your company is hired to repair a television transmitter and the repair is defective, you should expect to have to appear to defend yourself against any lawsuits related to your repair.

The issues become murkier when your company is sued for matters that don't arise directly from business that you do in the state. As a general rule, if your company is fairly active within a state, you will likely have to defend all type of lawsuits—even claims unrelated to business transacted within the state. This broader jurisdiction is known as general personal jurisdiction and is justified by a company's "substantial, continuous, and systematic" activity within the state.

EXAMPLE: A furniture making company, Quality Dinette, was incorporated in Alabama, where it maintained its offices. While at an Atlanta trade show, Quality Dinette entered into a deal to buy furniture making equipment from a company, SLI, and to have it shipped to Georgia and North Carolina. Later, a Michigan bank acquired the assets of SLI. When Quality Dinette didn't deliver on time, the Michigan bank sued Quality Dinette in Michigan. Quality Dinette had no property or offices in Michigan and did not advertise in Michigan. However the company had a sales rep in Michigan and sales of approximately $300,000 a year to Michigan customers.

Even though the lawsuit didn't arise from any sales or related activities by Quality Dinette in Michigan (and the contract was entered into in Atlanta), a Michigan court ruled that Quality Dinette was subject to general personal jurisdiction in Michigan. The judge ruled that the company's business was "substantial, continuous and systematic" based on the facts that Quality Dinette:

- retained an independent sales representative in Michigan
- conducted mail order solicitations of businesses in Michigan
- solicited sales from 122 businesses in Michigan in one year
- made 171 sales in Michigan totaling $279,557.32 in one year (approximately 3% of Quality Dinette's total sales that year)
- made 238 sales totaling $347,968.91 in Michigan in the year in which the transactions forming the basis of the lawsuit occurred, and
- made at least one sale in Michigan in each and every month over the two-year period of the lawsuit.

(*Michigan Nat'l Bank v. Quality Dinette, Inc.,* 888 F.2d 462 (6th Cir 1989).)

On the other hand, the less business you transact in a state, the more likely it is you will have to defend only a select or narrower range of activities—usually only those specifically arising from your activities in the state. This lower standard is known as limited personal jurisdiction. For example, if your only contact is the sale of bicycles to state residents, you would have to defend only lawsuits regarding the sale or use of the bicycles—not lawsuits brought by third parties, such as banks.

Can Officers, Agents, or Employees (or Parent, Subsidiary, or Successor Companies) Be Sued in Another State?

The fact that your company has minimum contacts with a state does not confer personal jurisdiction on others who work for or with your company. Officers, agents, and employees are all judged individually on the basis of their contacts with a state. Of course, any employees or agents who reside in that state will automatically be subject to personal jurisdiction there. In addition, less is required to establish personal jurisdiction if your employees or agents intentionally caused harm to another state's residents.

> EXAMPLE: Entertainer Shirley Jones, a California resident, sued the *National Enquirer*, a Florida corporation with its principal place of business in Florida, for defamation. There was no problem establishing personal jurisdiction in California over the *National Enquirer*. The newspaper advertised extensively in California and approximately 600,000 of its 5,000,000 weekly copies were sold there.
>
> Jones also sued the president and editor of the *National Enquirer* and the reporter who wrote the story, both residents of Florida. Even though they had little personal contact with the state of California, the two employees were subject to personal jurisdiction in California because they "calculated to cause injury" against Californian Shirley Jones. (*Calder v. Jones*, 465 U.S. 783 (1984).)

A judge usually will not impute personal jurisdiction to your company's parent company or a subsidiary company just because the state has jurisdiction over you. However, if your company uses the parent or subsidiary to provide services that are sufficiently important to the company, this will bring everyone within the umbrella of personal jurisdiction.

A company that acquires your business (a successor) may be liable for problems that occurred while you were running the business—for example, a breached contract or defective merchandise. In that case, the successor stands in your shoes—if you had minimum contacts, then so does your successor. This prevents corporations from avoiding jurisdiction simply by changing ownership. (*City of Richmond v. Madison Mtg. Group* (4th Cir. 1990) 918 F.2d 438.)

Can You Contract Your Way Out of Lawsuits in Another State?

A contract can specify where lawsuits between the contracting parties will occur. These provisions—sometimes called forum-selection or jurisdiction clauses—require that the parties consent in advance to the jurisdiction of a specific court, and that the parties waive the right to complain about jurisdiction later or bring a lawsuit anywhere else.

Forum-selection provisions affect only lawsuits arising out of or relating to the contract. If you include a forum-selection provision in a contract to supply computer repair services to a bank, your company would have to submit to personal jurisdiction over matters arising from your services with the bank only. The provision would not affect disputes with other clients (unless, of course, they had similar contractual provisions) or with the bank over matters not related to the contract.

Two states—Idaho and Montana—refuse to honor these provisions. In other states (Florida, for example), courts have required some contacts with the state beyond the existence of the contract provision. (*McRae v. J.D./M.D., Inc.,* 511 So.2d 540 (1987).) And in many state and federal lawsuits, you are not allowed to use forum-selection clauses for specific types of claims. For example, under Wisconsin law, a forum-selection clause in a contract to improve land is unenforceable. These laws are remnants of a legal tradition that believed that citizens should not be able to bargain for jurisdiction (sometimes referred to as forum shopping).

A judge will not enforce a forum-selection provision in a contract unless the contract was freely negotiated and the provision is not unreasonable and does not offend constitutional standards. In some circumstances, for example, these provisions may be void when used in a form contract that a consumer is unlikely to read or unable to negotiate (known as a contract of adhesion). In these situations, what is at issue is whether information about the provision was communicated to the consumer.

EXAMPLE: A skier purchased a lift ticket at a ski resort in Vermont. The terms of the agreement with the resort were printed on the back of the ticket, including a provision establishing that all lawsuits had to be brought in the state of Vermont. The skier was injured at the resort when he struck a pole. He sued in his state of residence, Connecticut, and the resort objected, stating that the case had to be brought in Vermont. The Connecticut court disagreed and found the existence of the forum-selection clause on a ski ticket was not a reasonable method of communicating the information to the skier. (*O'Brien v. Okemo Mt.*, 17 F. Supp.2d 98 (D. Conn. 1998).)

Forum-selection provisions are often overlooked during negotiations—relegated to the fine print category—and their full impact is usually not realized until months or years later.

EXAMPLE: A couple opened a Burger King franchise in Michigan. In their agreement with Burger King was a forum-selection clause in which they consented to jurisdiction in Florida. Later, when problems arose, the couple argued that it wasn't fair to have to travel to Florida and that they were not aware of the meaning of the provision. The courts upheld the jurisdiction clause, and the couple was forced to fight Burger King in Florida. (*Burger King Corp. v. Rudzewicz*, 471 U.S. 462 (1985).)

Don't confuse forum-selection provisions with governing law provisions. (See below.) Although the two may be combined in a contract, each establishes a separate requirement. A forum-selection provision sets out where a case can be filed (personal jurisdiction). A governing law provision sets out which state's laws will be used to make a decision in the dispute.

As a general rule, if you have sufficient bargaining power when entering into an agreement, include a forum-selection provision that establishes jurisdiction in your state of choice. If you cannot obtain jurisdiction where you want it, don't include any reference to jurisdiction in the agreement. In that case, the location of the case is usually determined by whoever files the lawsuit, assuming personal jurisdiction can be accomplished. A typical forum-selection provision would provide as follows:

Jurisdiction. Each party: (a) consents to the exclusive jurisdiction and venue of the federal and state courts located in San Francisco County, California, in any action arising out of or relating to this agreement; (b) waives any objection it might have to jurisdiction or venue of such forums or that the forum is inconvenient; and (c) agrees not to bring any such action in any other jurisdiction or venue to which either party might be entitled by domicile or otherwise.

Which State's Laws Apply With an Out-of-State Dispute?

Normally, the laws of the forum state (the state in which the lawsuit is filed) are applied in a dispute. However, this rule may vary depending on the nature of the dispute and where it arose. For example, in contract disputes, some state courts may choose the state with the most significant relationship to the contract.

The choice of law can have a significant impact. For example, you might be sued about something where the statute of limitations (the law setting the time limits for when a certain type of case can be filed) has expired in your home state, but not in the state where the lawsuit is filed.

If you successfully argue that your state's laws should apply, the lawsuit couldn't be brought, because the time for filing the suit would have passed. On that basis, you decide to fight over whether the other state has personal jurisdiction over your company.

It is possible to add a provision in a contract determining which state's laws should be chosen in a future dispute (known as a choice of law provision). An example of a governing law provision is:

Governing Law. Each party agrees that the laws of the State of Massachusetts govern all matters arising out of or relating to this Agreement.

Courts will usually uphold such provisions unless they are found unreasonable or violate a state statute that prohibits their use in certain instances.

For most basic contract and corporate matters, state laws are fairly similar. However, some states are centers for certain industries, and their laws may be more geared to a particular industry's interests. For example, publishers tend to prefer the laws of New York, software and motion picture companies prefer the laws of California, and oil and gas companies often prefer the state laws of Texas and Oklahoma. If you are concerned about the choice of laws, consult with an attorney before entering into a contract.

CAUTION

A choice of law provision can affect whether a court will make you appear to defend a lawsuit in another state. For example, if you include a choice of law provision designating New York law, a New York court may take that into account when determining whether New York has personal jurisdiction over your company. After all, if you agree ahead of time to use New York law in a dispute, that demonstrates some association with the state. Conversely, if a foreign company negotiates an agreement that includes a choice of English law, that would weigh against establishing personal jurisdiction over the company in a Texas court. (*Jones v. Petty-Ray Geophysical Geosource, Inc.* 954 F.2d 1061 (5th Cir. 1992).)

Should You Fight Personal Jurisdiction?

When a lawsuit is filed against your company, no one at the courthouse will ask about personal jurisdiction or how much business your company has done with the forum state. But sometimes you can prevent things from going any further. Once you are served with the lawsuit—either in person, through your agent for service, or by any of the other methods authorized by the court—you can object and request that the court dismiss the case.

Unfortunately, this requires time and expense. You'll need to hire an attorney to file paperwork asking the court to get rid of the lawsuit (known as a motion to dismiss). Your attorney will argue that it is unfair, under the Constitution's due process standards, for you to have to travel to that state and defend the lawsuit there. In other words, you will argue that the state does not have personal jurisdiction over your company.

Once you file a motion to dismiss the case, a court will engage in a two-step analysis. First, the court must determine whether the state long-arm statute authorizes jurisdiction over your company. Second, the court must consider whether the exercise of personal jurisdiction would deny your company its constitutional right to due process of law. During this analysis, the court determines whether your company has sufficient contacts with the forum state.

When the court rules on your motion to dismiss, it will either establish personal jurisdiction or dismiss the case. If the court establishes personal jurisdiction and you disagree with the decision, you can appeal the court's decision. Many litigants have taken these cases all the way to the U.S. Supreme Court. There are risks to appealing, however.

While you appeal the jurisdictional issue, the underlying case proceeds (except in the unlikely event the case is stayed or delayed during the appeal process). Because you have refused to submit to jurisdiction, you can't defend yourself in the case and will therefore likely end up with a default judgment entered against you. Unless you win your jurisdiction argument—usually an uphill battle—the default judgment can be enforced against you in states where you have assets. So you take a substantial risk when you appeal a jurisdiction decision, because you automatically lose the underlying suit. And appealing a personal jurisdiction decision is expensive; you could spend more money appealing the decision than you would by losing the underlying lawsuit.

If you choose to ignore a lawsuit that is filed against you in another state, the court in the forum state will most likely award a default judgment to the party that sued your company. With the judgment in hand, they can chase your company around the country and enforce the judgment—that is, get a local court to help collect the money from your company.

CAUTION

The rules of personal jurisdiction also apply to federal courts in other states. If you are sued in federal court, personal jurisdiction must be established within the state in which the federal court is located before you can be forced to defend yourself in an out-of-state federal court. There are certain exceptions to this general rule—for example, for companies in federally regulated commerce.

Can You Sue Employees or Independent Contractors in Other States?

If your company pays people who work and are located in another state, it's important to know whether these people are employees or independent contractors. This distinction can have a major impact on whether you will be able to bring a lawsuit against these people in that state.

If you have employees in another state, you generally must qualify to do business in that state. If they are independent contractors, you are less likely to have these obligations. For example, if your company maintains an office with an employee in another state, you would most likely be engaged in intrastate commerce and required to register as a foreign corporation in that state. With an independent contractor, on the other hand, you are less likely to be engaged in the degree of business that would require you to register as a foreign corporation.

If you fail to qualify in a state where you have an employee, you could be prevented from bringing a lawsuit against the employee in that state. This may seem like a drastic result—a company is prevented from suing an employee—but it is not uncommon.

EXAMPLE: A Michigan corporation, L.C. Dortch, Inc., manufactured and sold laundry and dry cleaning equipment. The corporation employed a full-time sales manager who maintained an office in Ohio. The salesman solicited business but did not finalize the sales, set prices, or service the equipment—these matters were all completed through the Michigan office. The company became embroiled in a dispute with the sales manager and sued him in Ohio. An Ohio judge dismissed the case. Why? The judge determined that the salesman was an employee, not an independent contractor. By maintaining an office with an employee, the judge decided that Dortch was doing the degree of business in Ohio that required registering as a foreign corporation. But Dortch had failed to register, because it mistakenly believed that the manager was a contractor, not an employee. Because the company failed to qualify to do business, it could not sue the manager in Ohio. (*L.C. Dortch, Inc. v. Goldstein*, 200 N.E.2d 828 (1964).)

The status of your workers matters not just for purposes of doing business out of state but also for purposes of federal income taxes, state unemployment compensation, state income taxes, workers' compensation, overtime, and ownership of your intellectual property.

> **CAUTION**
>
> **Be careful when you classify workers as employees or independent contractors.** There are several different tests for determining whether someone you hire is an employee or an independent contractor. For information on how to classify workers, see *Working With Independent Contractors,* by Stephen Fishman (Nolo).

Internet Issues

Consider this possibility: Your company, incorporated and based in Massachusetts, manufactures atomic clocks. Your website business has been slow, so you pay for a California company to revamp and host your website. You contract with a New York public relations company to spread the word about your business. Within weeks of going live with your new look and promotion, sales triple. Wow! You proudly announce in your company newsletter that, for the first time, you're doing business in 50 states.

Aside from the sales fanfare and increased revenues, do your spreading sales, California Web hosting, and New York public relations also mean that you must collect sales taxes or qualify to do business in other states? Will you have to defend your company in the state of Washington if a consumer there is shocked when plugging their clock into an outlet?

The answer to the first question regarding taxes and qualifying to do business is: No. In general, the rules for Internet-based businesses are the same as the rules for other companies discussed above. The answer to the second question about defending lawsuits is: Probably. There is still some uncertainty and confusion regarding Internet business transactions and personal jurisdiction—that is, when an Internet-based business must defend itself in another state.

When Do You Generally Have to Pay Sales Tax for Internet Sales?

For now, if your company has a website, you do not have to collect or pay sales taxes to a state unless you have a physical presence in that state—that is, your company maintains its inventory there, rents or owns real property, maintains employees, or directly provides services within the state. For example, an Internet bookseller that maintains a warehouse in California would have to pay sales taxes on sales initiated by California residents. This may seem like you're hearing the same rule over and over—and you are—but there is one twist when it comes to Internet sales taxes: Things are changing

State governments are in desperate need of money. Approximately one-third of all states' revenues (which currently amount to about $150 billion) come from sales taxes. These taxes pay for everything from schools, fire departments, and police to roads, parks, and other state services. States that don't have a personal income tax (like Texas) are even more dependent on sales tax revenue. (There are five states that don't have a sales tax: Alaska, Delaware, Montana, New Hampshire, and Oregon.)

In 1998, Congress passed the Internet Tax Freedom Act (ITFA), which established a moratorium on new state and local taxes of Internet access service and also established a ban on new taxes on e-commerce. In 2003, the act expired, making it possible for new tax rules to surface. In recent years, some large retailers entered into an agreement with various states and the District of Columbia to voluntarily collect taxes on their Internet sales. Forty-four states have cooperated to support the Streamlined Sales and Use Tax (and as of 2010, 21 states had adopted the act as law), which would simplify and harmonize uniform sales and use tax collection and administration by retailers and states. Some states have taken an alternative approach. For example, in June 2008, the state of New York began collecting sales tax from Amazon.com, even though Seattle-based Amazon had no warehouses or stores in New York. Instead, the state argued that many of the Amazon associates—retailers who sell goods through Amazon—are in New York. Amazon is currently battling that decision. And in June 2010, yet another attempt at revising the Internet sales tax rules—The Main Street Fairness Act—was introduced.

Generally, for now, you are only legally obligated to pay sales taxes when you have a physical presence in a sales tax state. But those rules may change. To stay current, check websites, such as the Sales Tax Institute (www.salestaxinstitute.com) and E-Commerce Tax News (www.ecommercetax.com).

The *Borders* Decision: The Shape of Things to Come?

In a California case (*Borders Online, LLC v. State Bd. of Equalization* (2005) 129 Cal.4th 1179, 29 CR3d 176), an appeals court decided that even though Borders Online, LLC, was a Delaware business with no physical presence in California, and even though the LLC was a separate entity from the brick-and-mortar Borders storefronts located throughout the state, sales of books on the website were subject to California use tax. The reason? The website publicizes a refund policy that allows online customers to obtain a refund or return merchandise credit at any retail store located in the state. This transactional "nexus" between the online sales and the storefront refund/credit policy was enough to make the online sales by Borders subject to California state use taxes.

New State Use Tax Collection Procedures

Technically, state sales tax is owed on tangible personal property purchased and used within a state. State use tax is owed on property purchased out of state and used *in* the state. In the past, most states ignored the collection of use tax except on out-of-state sales of big ticket items, such as cars, boats, planes, etc. Now that many states are facing significant budget deficits, they are adopting broader and more aggressive use tax collection procedures. For example, California now requires service-type businesses with $100,000 or more in annual gross receipts to file annual state use tax returns that are used to report and pay use tax on all tangible personal property bought out of state or online and used in the business. We expect other states to adopt similar procedures in their attempt to add use tax revenue to their coffers.

What If Your Servers or Web Design Services Are in Another State?

Leasing or paying for the use of servers—the computers that host a company's website—is not considered doing business for purposes of qualification or taxes. The same is true for hiring a design firm in another state. However, these dealings could require you to appear to defend a lawsuit in another state if a dispute arises out of your agreement with the hosting or design company. For example, if your Web design team sues you for payment in its home state of Oregon, you may have to defend that lawsuit there. Be aware, jurisdiction in these cases is often determined by forum selection provisions in the hosting or design agreements.

Where Must You Qualify If Your Company Operates a Website?

The fact that a state's residents can access or purchase from your website is not, by itself, enough to require you to qualify in that state. Unless your company has a presence there in some other way, you will not have to qualify to do business in that state. For example, if your company maintains fulfillment centers in other states, it will probably have to qualify in the states where the orders are filled.

> EXAMPLE: FelliniDVD.com, incorporated in Pennsylvania, rents foreign DVDs to subscribers in all 50 states. For years, the company received orders and shipped DVDs at its Pennsylvania headquarters and did not have to qualify to do business anywhere else. As subscriptions increased, the company opened a fulfillment center in Nevada to fill orders from its West Coast customers. FelliniDVD must now qualify to do business (and pay taxes) in Nevada.

What About Downloadable Products?

If visitors to your website can purchase downloadable products from your site, such as books or music, this activity alone shouldn't subject you to registration requirements. However, offering downloadable products for sale may subject you to lawsuits in the states where your customers have placed their orders. That's because when a company profits directly from a state's residents, courts are more willing to require the company to defend itself in that state.

If Your Company Operates a Website, Where Can It Be Sued?

The rules about when your company must defend a lawsuit in another state boil down to fairness. Basically, you have to travel to other states when your business causes an injury in that state or when you have sufficient business contacts in that state (the minimum-contacts requirement).

In determining whether it's fair to impose personal jurisdiction on an out-of-state Internet-based company, courts will look for activity in the state that is continuous and systematic. For example, an Internet service provider that has thousands of subscribers and advertises heavily in the state would have the type of presence that would justify bringing the company into court.

EXAMPLE 1: A Pennsylvania court was able to obtain personal jurisdiction over a California Internet service provider that had 3,000 Pennsylvania subscribers. The act of processing the Pennsylvania applications and assigning passwords was sufficient to demonstrate the minimum contacts needed for personal jurisdiction. (*Zippo Mfg. Co. v. Zippo Dot Com, Inc.*, 952 F. Supp. 1119 (W.D. Pa. 1997).)

EXAMPLE 2: A Texas court obtained personal jurisdiction over an out-of-state online gambling enterprise because the gambling operation entered into contracts with Texas residents to play online gambling games, sent emails to the Texas residents, and sent winnings to Texas residents. (*Thompson v. Handa-Lopez, Inc.*, 998 F. Supp. 738 (W.D. Tex. 1998).)

The two most common reasons for requiring an Internet company to appear in an out-of-state court—minimum contacts and causing an injury—are described in more detail below.

The Passive/Interactive/Active Standard

Personal jurisdiction based on Internet activities is a tricky issue. However, a website must do more than simply exist to subject its owners to personal jurisdiction. Otherwise, website owners would be subject to personal jurisdiction in every state simply because their website is viewable there. An Idaho-based consulting company with a website, for example, would not have to defend itself in Rhode Island just because Rhode Island residents can access its website.

State and federal courts have adopted a sliding scale measuring an Internet company's contact with state residents to help determine jurisdiction. At one end of the scale are passive sites: websites that merely post information. No sales are made or other type of active business engaged in from these websites. Because there is less contact with the forum state, passive sites are unlikely to incur personal jurisdiction—except in the state where the owner resides or does other business.

EXAMPLE 1: A Minnesota nutrition supplement company maintained a website but did not sell its products directly over the Internet. Instead, it directed consumers to email the company's distributors. A Texas nutrition company sued the Minnesota company in Texas for patent infringement. A court ruled that the Minnesota site was passive and there were insufficient contacts with Texas to give the court personal jurisdiction over the company. (*Nutrition Physiology Corp. v. Enviros Ltd.*, 87 F. Supp. 2d 648 (N.D. Texas 2000).)

EXAMPLE 2: A Missouri jazz club's website offered information but did not sell goods or services online to website users. The site was found to be passive, with insufficient contacts to New York (the forum state) to justify New York courts considering a lawsuit against the club. (*Bensusan Restaurant Corp. v. King*, 937 F. Supp. 295 (S.D. N.Y. 1996).)

At the other end of the sliding scale are interactive sites: websites where credit card sales or other active business is conducted. These websites are more likely to satisfy the minimum-contacts requirement because of interaction—through sales or services provided—between the company and the forum state.

EXAMPLE 1: A California man running a website called nfltoday.com earned revenue from his website by advertising, specifically through the sale of sports betting ads. The site was generating substantial income through interstate commerce and was disrupting marketing efforts by the National Football League in New York. When the NFL sued for trademark infringement, a court determined that the site was not passive and that the enterprise had sufficient contacts with New York State to justify jurisdiction. (*National Football League v. Miller,* 105 F. Supp.2d 131 (S.D. N.Y. 2000).)

EXAMPLE 2: The Mayo Clinic website solicited medical business from Texas residents. Specifically, Mayo provided directions for doctors to refer patients to the clinic, provided a toll-free number, and had treated approximately 1,000 Texas residents in the five years preceding the lawsuit. A court ruled that the site was interactive and Mayo had sufficient contacts with Texas (the forum state) to justify a Texas court's hearing the case. (*Mayo Clinic v. Jackson,* 1998 Tex. App. LEXIS 6307 (Tex. App. 1998).)

The fact that a website is interactive is not enough, by itself, to subject a company to personal jurisdiction in every state. There must also be some interaction—such as sales or services—between the company and the forum state.

EXAMPLE: A South Carolina company sold music CDs and the like through its retail outlet and its website. An Oregon music store with a similar name sued the South Carolina company in Oregon. Although the South Carolina website was interactive—consumers could buy directly from the site—the court dismissed the case for lack of personal jurisdiction. It was not enough that the site was interactive; the company had not made any sales to Oregon residents and had made "no deliberate and repeated contacts" with Oregon. (*Millennium Enterprises, Inc. v. Millennium Music, L.P.,* 33 F. Supp.2d 907 (D. Or. 1999).)

Between these two extremes—passive and interactive websites—is a broad middle ground: websites that allow some information to be exchanged between the company and the user but don't rise to the level of actively doing business. For example, some websites provide an email address to request product information. Applying the sliding scale becomes more difficult in these situations.

Banner Ads = Doing Business?

Running another company's advertisements on your website will not, by itself, make you have to register to do business or pay sales tax to another state. However, it can be a factor in determining whether you may be forced to defend yourself in a lawsuit in another state. Remember, the chances that you'll have to answer to another state's courts depend on how extensive your contacts are with that state—and the revenue generated by ads may add up to sufficient contacts.

Internet advertising triggers revenue in two ways. First, your company is earning money from the advertiser—either through direct payments or payments contingent upon click-through sales. Second, the advertiser is indirectly using your site to generate sales with out-of-state residents. In other words, even if your site is relatively passive, having third-party advertisements may create sufficient contacts with another state.

In one case, a website owner was sued over trademark infringement and forced to defend itself in New York. One factor in the decision was the substantial revenue from New York residents generated by the company's third-party banner ads. (*National Football League v. Miller,* 105 F. Supp.2d 131 (S.D. N.Y. 2000).)

Causing a Tort Within the State

A person who commits a tort (a type of legal claim that causes damage or injury) can be sued and required to appear in the state where he or she committed the tort—even if the tort is the sole contact with the forum state. Similar rules apply for Internet companies that commit torts, except that it's not enough that an injury was caused by the Internet activity—courts also look for evidence that the activity was "purposefully directed" at the forum state.

> EXAMPLE 1: A New Mexico software company sent defamatory email and made defamatory Web postings about an Arizona company. An Arizona court imposed personal jurisdiction because the defamatory statements were intentionally aimed at an Arizona business and caused an injury (defamation) within the state. (*EDIAS Software Intern. v. BASIS Intern., Ltd.* 947 F. Supp. 412 (D. Ariz. 1996).)

> EXAMPLE 2: Matt Drudge of The Drudge Report, a gossip website, made alleged defamatory statements about a Washington, DC, resident on the Drudge Report website. Although Drudge lived and wrote his column in California, a court ruled that he was subject to personal jurisdiction in the District of Columbia because the injury occurred in the District of Columbia and Drudge had sufficient contacts with the District of Columbia. Namely, he emailed his column to a list of District of Columbia email addresses, he solicited contributions and collected money from District of Columbia residents, he traveled to the District of Columbia twice to promote his column, and District of Columbia residents systematically supplied Drudge with the fodder for his business: gossip. (*Blumenthal v. Drudge,* 992 F. Supp. 44 (D. D.C 1998).) ●

PART

2

Converting a Sole Proprietorship to Another Entity

I f you could choose a business entity and stick with it for the course of your business's life, you could minimize paperwork, save legal expenses, and make financial and tax planning more predictable. For a variety of reasons, however, many businesses must convert from one entity to another. Sometimes success is the motivator—for example, a partnership might incorporate to allow eager investors to buy preferred shares in the new corporation. Sometimes, a business changes form in order to adjust to new circumstances—for example, if you are the only remaining member of a partnership, you change over to a sole owner LLC.

This chapter explores available legal and tax migration paths and procedures for the sole proprietorship. Subsequent chapters explain how to convert partnerships, LLCs, and C and S corporations to different business forms.

Converting a Sole Proprietorship to a Partnership

This chapter starts by explaining the procedures for, and consequences of, converting a sole proprietorship to a partnership. This is one of the most common conversions and happens automatically when the sole owner of a business brings in another owner. The rules set forth below are for general partnerships. Some different procedures and rules apply to limited partnerships, as noted throughout this section.

 RELATED TOPIC

General vs. limited partnerships. For an explanation of the differences between general and limited partnerships, see Chapter 1.

TIP

Consider forming an LLC instead of a partnership. When you bring in a second owner, you might want to create an LLC. The LLC gives each owner the extra advantage of limited liability protection—that is, protection against personal liability for business debts and claims. This extra protection can be comforting when you add another owner to your business, because a new partner can subject your business (and you) to liability for his or her business decisions and contracts. Later in this chapter, we explain how to convert a sole proprietorship to an LLC.

Legal Procedures

A one-person business automatically becomes a general partnership when a second owner is brought into the business. You don't have to file any paperwork with the state to make this change. Once you bring another owner on board, you've formed a partnership.

However, the partners in the new business should take a few steps to put their house in order:

- **Prepare a partnership agreement.** Partners should prepare and sign a partnership agreement to document how they have agreed to divide ownership interests, profits, losses, and voting and liquidation rights, and to spell out the rights and responsibilities of the partners.

RESOURCE

Want help creating a partnership agreement? For information on forming a partnership and drafting an agreement, see *Form a Partnership*, by Ralph Warner and Denis Clifford (Nolo).

- **Revise licenses, permits, and registrations.** The partners may need to revise and update government paperwork in the name of the new partnership. This could include professional, state, and local licenses;

state sales and use tax permits; and government registrations. If the partnership will operate under a name other than the surnames of the partners, it must file a new fictitious business name registration.

- **Get an EIN.** The partnership should get a new federal employer identification number (EIN), even if it doesn't have employees. (Partners who receive a share of the profits are not considered employees for payroll tax purposes.) The EIN must be used on partnership tax returns.

In addition, the partnership should cancel any licenses and other papers in the name of the sole proprietorship.

TIP

Converting to a limited partnership. A sole proprietor can convert a sole proprietorship to a limited partnership by filing a certificate of limited partnership with the state filing office (typically, the secretary of state). When making this type of conversion, the sole proprietor typically continues to serve as the general partner and manager of the business (and is personally liable for business debts and claims), while one or more limited partners join solely to invest in the business.

Income Tax Consequences of Conversion

There are no immediate income tax consequences when a sole proprietorship converts to a partnership: The sole proprietor contributes the assets of the existing proprietorship to the new partnership, while the new co-owner contributes cash or other property. Thanks to Section 721(a) of the Internal Revenue Code, this is normally not considered a taxable event; that is, it is a "tax-neutral" change rather than a taxable sale or exchange under federal and state tax law.

In some situations, however, the conversion may trigger taxation. When a partnership issues a "capital interest" to a partner in return for the past or future performance of *services,* it may be a taxable event. A capital interest is an interest in the assets of the partnership that is later paid to the owner if he or she withdraws from the partnership or the partnership liquidates. If a capital interest is issued for past or future services, the value of the interest will immediately be taxed as service income. The government taxes the partner rendering the services as though the partnership had paid him or her right away, rather than promising to pay in the future.

> **EXAMPLE:** Bob owns a successful sole proprietorship but needs help running the business. He asks John to join him as an equal partner in return for entering into a ten-year full-time employment contract. John hires an independent appraiser to value the business. The appraiser says a half-interest currently is worth $150,000. To avoid having to pay tax immediately on $150,000 (the value of the half-interest), John decides instead to purchase the half-interest outright, in exchange for some cash and a promissory note to pay the partnership the remaining balance over time. John enters into a separate employment contract with the partnership, which is not tied to his purchase of half of the company.

Because of this exception for capital interests, a partner who performs or agrees to perform services for the partnership usually either:

- chooses to take a share of the earnings and profits of the partnership —a transaction that normally is not taxed—instead of a capital interest, or
- buys the interest under other terms (in other words, for cash, property, or a promissory note—not for services to the partnership).

Another strategy to avoid triggering taxes in this situation is to characterize the services to be provided as a capital contribution of "know-how," which is considered property rather than services. Make sure your tax adviser is comfortable with this strategy before you use it—and carefully document the nature and value of the "know-how" in case the IRS raises questions during a later audit of your business or the owner.

Some Special Tax Exceptions

In most cases, it's hard to estimate how large a partnership's future profit payouts will be, so profits interests in a partnership are usually not taxed until the partnership earns profits and allocates them to the partner. So, a partner usually won't be taxed if he or she receives a profits interest—rather than a capital interest—in a partnership in return for services.

However, if the partnership's profits can reliably be calculated in advance—that is, if the partner can reasonably predict what profits will be—the partner *will* be taxed on the value of the profits interest. In addition, the service partner must pay taxes on the profits interest if it is sold or transferred within two years of the grant. Finally, under proposed Treasury Regulation 105346-03, partnerships and their owners must follow special rules, adopt special agreements, and make sure that special tax elections are filed by persons receiving profits interests within 30 days of the issuance of the interests to obtain favorable tax treatment of that interest. Make sure to ask your tax adviser how to comply with these and the other special rules and requirements associated with issuing profits interests before you decide to issue profits interests in return for the performance of services.

Finally, here's another exception to the tax-free conversion rules: The IRS will tax the conversion of a sole proprietorship to a partnership if the sole proprietor goes about it in a nontraditional way. For example, if, instead of contributing all the assets of the sole proprietorship directly to the new partnership, the sole proprietor personally sells half of the sole proprietorship assets to the new co-owner, and then each contributes their one-half share of assets to the new partnership, there may be tax consequences.

In this situation, the sole proprietor must pay income taxes on any gain from the initial sale of assets to the other person. Specifically, there will be a taxable gain to the sole proprietor if the selling price of the one-half interest in assets is more than the sole proprietor's income tax basis in these assets.

Some Special Tax Exceptions (cont'd)

For more information about the different tax results that can occur when a one-owner business is converted to a two-owner business, see Revenue Ruling 99-5. (Type "Revenue Ruling 99-5" into your search engine.) Although the ruling talks about the conversion of a one-owner LLC to a co-owned LLC, it applies to the conversion of a sole proprietorship to a partnership, too.

Tax Filing Procedures

After a sole proprietorship is converted to a partnership, the owners must file IRS Form 1065, *U.S. Return of Partnership Income,* at the end of each tax year. The partnership also must prepare a 1065 Schedule K-1, *Partner's Share of Income, Deductions, Credits, etc.,* to give to each partner. The K-1 shows the amount of income or loss, deductions, credits, and other tax-related items each partner must report on his or her individual 1040 tax return.

The basic income tax treatment of profits earned in the business remains the same. Partners, like sole proprietors, report and pay income tax on all profits earned each year in the business, whether or not the company actually pays out profits to the partners.

Partners are not considered employees for payroll tax purposes.

Partnership Tax Law Can Be Complex

If you are used to doing your own financial record keeping and tax preparation as a sole proprietor, expect your job to get a lot harder once you form a partnership. The IRS 1065 Partnership return requires you to prepare financial statements such as a balance sheet and a listing of the income, losses, gains, deductions, and credits the partnership generated.

To pull together this data, normally the business must maintain a well organized double-entry accounting system geared to a partnership business, which typically includes daily journals and a general ledger, to keep track of the items and amounts that must be reported on the year-end partnership tax return. The issues and ambiguities that arise in partnership tax law and practice are numerous. In fact, many tax practitioners believe partnership taxation is even more complicated than corporate taxation, because it offers more wiggle room to bend and custom tailor the rules. The bottom line is that you will need to hire an experienced partnership tax adviser to help you get your financial books and accounting procedures in place and to prepare the partnership's tax return and tax schedules each year.

Self-Employment Taxes

Converting a sole proprietorship to a partnership does not change the self-employment tax status of the business owner. Before and after the conversion, net profits from the business are treated as earned income of the owners, who must pay self-employment taxes on this amount.

> **TIP**
>
> **Limited partners don't owe self-employment tax on profits.**
> If you form a limited partnership, investors brought into the business as
> limited partners won't have to pay self-employment tax on profits allocated
> to them. However, any partner who is active in the business and earns an
> income will owe self-employment tax on that amount.

Securities Laws Procedures

Federal and state laws define a "security" as an interest that is purchased with the expectation of earning profits from the activities of others. These laws generally don't apply when you convert a sole proprietorship to a partnership. Even though the sale of ownership interests—including the exchange of money or property for ownership that occurs when a partnership is formed—is regulated by federal and state securities laws, these laws apply when the buyer of the interest expects to earn profits from the work of others. Because each member of a general partnership has management power and actively runs or is responsible for the business, each partner is producing profits from his or her own efforts, not earning profits from the activities of others. Therefore, these laws normally don't apply to partnership sales of interests to general partners.

> **CAUTION**
>
> **Limited partners may be subject to securities laws.** Issuing
> partnership interests is usually exempt from securities laws; however,
> the rules are different when you form a limited partnership. A limited
> partnership interest qualifies as a security—an ownership interest purchased
> with the expectation of profiting from someone else's work—under state
> and federal securities laws, and the sale of limited partnership interests
> must comply with these laws. For contact information for the agency that
> administers securities in your state, see the appendix.

Converting a Sole Proprietorship to an LLC

A sole proprietor can convert to an LLC in most states with a modest amount of paperwork and fees, and with no change to the owner's income tax treatment and filing requirements. That said, there are numerous exceptions and strategies that affect a sole proprietor's conversion to an LLC. This section explains the conversion process, including what happens if one or more owners join the business at the time of conversion.

 RESOURCE

Find out how to form an LLC. For more information and step-by-step instructions on forming an LLC, read *Form Your Own Limited Liability Company*, by Anthony Mancuso (Nolo).

Legal Procedures

Every state allows you to form an LLC with just one member (owner), so a sole proprietor can convert his or her one-person business to an LLC. However, a sole proprietor can also bring additional owners into the business when converting to an LLC.

Here are the steps required to change a sole proprietorship to an LLC:

- **File articles of organization.** The owner(s) must file LLC articles of organization with the state filing office (typically, the corporations division of the secretary of state's office).

- **Prepare an LLC operating agreement.** The new owner(s) should create an LLC operating agreement documenting ownership interests, profits, losses, voting and liquidation rights, and the other rights and responsibilities of the members. Even a one-owner LLC should have an operating agreement—because preparing one helps show that the owner takes management responsibilities seriously. This will help, if the need arises, to defeat efforts by your creditors or opponents in a lawsuit to "pierce the veil" of limited liability and go after your personal assets to satisfy your company's liabilities. (For more information, see "Piercing the Veil," in Chapter 2.)

- **Revise licenses, permits, and registrations.** The new entity should obtain new permits, licenses, and registrations in the name of the LLC and cancel licenses and permits taken out in the name of the now defunct sole proprietorship. If the LLC will do business under a name different from the LLC name specified in its articles of organization, it should file a fictitious business name statement.

- **Get an EIN.** A single-owner LLC is not required to obtain an employer identification number (EIN) unless the LLC will have employees or the sole owner establishes a retirement plan (such as a Keogh plan). However, if the sole proprietor brings in another owner when the business is converted to an LLC, the LLC will be treated as a partnership for tax purposes and *must* obtain an EIN to prepare its tax returns. An EIN is required even if the co-owned LLC has no employees and no retirement plans.

> **TIP**
> **LLC profits are not subject to withholding.** An LLC owner is not considered an employee, so employee income tax withholding doesn't apply. Of course, the owner must personally report and pay income tax on profits allocated to him or her and on any other income the owner receives from his or her LLC.

Income Tax Consequences of Conversion

The tax consequences of converting a sole proprietorship to an LLC are basically the same as for converting a sole proprietorship to a partnership. Like a conversion to a partnership, the IRS (and state tax authorities) normally treats the event only as a change in the form of the business, not as a taxable sale or exchange of the assets of the business.

This same tax-free rule also applies to the formation of a multiowner LLC. Even if you bring on additional owners at the time of the conversion, the event is typically treated as a tax-free transaction.

As always, there are exceptions to the tax-free conversion rule. In the previous section "Converting a Sole Proprietorship to a Partnership," we explained what happens when a partner is granted an interest in the new entity in exchange for services. Those same rules apply here as well. An LLC member who receives a capital (ownership) interest in an LLC in return for providing services is taxed on the value of these services, that is, the value of his or her ownership share in the business—even though the owner does not really receive any cash payment for services in the exchange.

Happily, you can avoid this taxation when you convert to an LLC with new members, just as you can when you convert to a partnership:

- The LLC can give an owner who provides services an LLC profits interest only, entitling that owner to a share of LLC profits but not granting voting, liquidation, or other membership rights.

- The LLC may characterize the capital contribution of its new member as a "know-how" contribution of knowledge and development expertise—an intangible item of personal property that is not taxable.

- The LLC service provider can buy the interest for cash or a promise to pay cash in the future, rather than for services.

If you use any of these tactics, be sure to consult a tax adviser to help you document your strategy, and make sure your LLC operating agreement accurately reflects the profits-interest or know-how capital contribution of the new member.

Finally, look at "Some Special Tax Exceptions," in the section "Converting a Sole Proprietorship to a Partnership," above. Those rules apply to the formation of LLCs as well as partnerships.

Tax Filing Procedures

For the most part, there are no special income tax provisions for sole proprietorships that convert to LLCs. Single-owner LLCs are treated as sole proprietorships for purposes of federal income tax reporting and payment; co-owned LLCs are treated as partnerships. Therefore, converting a sole proprietorship to a one-owner LLC does not change the owner's tax obligations. The sole LLC owner continues to report profits and losses on his or her Schedule C, *Profit or Loss From Business*.

When a sole proprietorship is converted to a multiowner LLC—that is, when new owners are added at the time of conversion—the co-owned LLC must follow federal partnership tax return requirements. It must file an IRS Form 1065, *U.S. Return of Partnership Income*, and prepare a Schedule K-1, *Partner's Share of Income, Deductions, Credits, etc.*, to give to each LLC member (owner). Members use the K-1 information to report their share of LLC profits on their 1040 individual income tax returns.

As with partners, LLC members are not considered employees for payroll tax purposes.

EXAMPLE: Rich is a keyboard player and the sole owner of "Eclectic Electric—A Found Sound Ensemble." Even though it's billed as an ensemble, Rich is the sole member of the band. His two-handed keyboard dexterity and skillful use of multitracked sampled sounds go over well at local venues. Rich decides to add a few other live musicians to the mix. He knows that there is a remote, yet real, possibility that someone in the band could be financially liable to others as a result of contract disputes, missed performances, hurled projectiles at performances, mosh pit incidents, and the like. He decides to convert his sole proprietorship to "Eclectic Electric, LLC" (and also adopt "EEL" as the new fictitious business name for the band). He wants to join forces with Tony and Lulu, accomplished local musicians who share his musical aesthetic, but he doesn't want to commit himself to putting them on salary as EEL employees. Nor does he want to make the new band members "instant owners" by giving them a capital interest in EEL. Instead, he offers each of them a 25% profits interest in the new band. This allows Rich to keep sole ownership of his band's name and goodwill while offering the new members a reasonable monetary stake in the future success of the group. The new band members will not be taxed on their profits interests until profits are actually allocated and paid out to them (the LLC operating agreement provides that all net profits get calculated and distributed on a monthly basis). This arrangement makes everyone happy.

CAUTION

Some states impose LLC tax return filing requirements and fees. Most states treat an LLC as the IRS does—as a sole proprietorship if the LLC has one owner, or a partnership if it has more than one owner. However, some states impose special requirements for LLC tax returns and annual taxes or fees. If you convert a sole proprietorship to an LLC in one of these states, your annual state tax or fee payments may change. For example, the California Franchise Tax Board requires LLCs that are formed or earn income in California to file Form 568, *Limited Liability Company Return of Income*, and pay an $800 minimum tax each year, plus an additional annual fee if the LLC's gross receipts exceed certain thresholds. For more information on special LLC fee and tax rules that apply in your state, see your state's business filing office website. (See the appendix.)

Self-Employment Taxes

Whether or not members of an LLC are subject to self-employment tax depends on whether the LLC operates under member-management or manager-management. Member-managed LLCs are managed by all the owners, but state laws also permit manager-management, in which the LLC is run by one or more specially appointed managers Under manager-management, one or more persons typically assume full-time control of the LLC, while the remaining owners act as "passive" investors.

For LLCs that are member-managed, the profits allocated to each member are considered earned income, subject to self-employment tax. However, in a manager-managed LLC, profits allocated to the designated individual managers should be subject to self-employment tax (because these managers are active in the business), while profits allocated to nonmanaging members should not be subject to self-employment tax.

This discussion uses the words "should" and "should not" because self-employment tax rules for LLCs are derived by analogy to existing rules for partnerships. The IRS has not provided any clear authority on how members and managers are treated for self-employment tax purposes. Check with your tax adviser for the latest and most authoritative information on LLC self-employment tax rules.

Securities Laws Procedures

As long as each LLC member is active in the business (as is the case in a member-managed LLC), his or her interest should not be considered a security under federal and state securities laws. However, in a manager-managed LLC, the sale of LLC interests probably will be considered a sale of securities under the federal and state rules.

In a manager-managed LLC, the nonmanaging members are investing with the expectation of earning profits from the efforts of others—the classic definition of a "security." The bottom line is this: Unless all sales are clearly exempt under an exception to federal or state securities law, a manager-managed LLC should qualify its sales of *all* LLC interests— those issued to both members and managers alike—under federal and state securities laws.

 CAUTION

Some states take an all-or-nothing approach to LLC securities regulation. Some states, like California, categorically say that unless all members manage your LLC, you must treat all sales of LLC interests, even sales to managing members, as "securities." This is a conservative approach but a safe rule to follow—which is why it's suggested above. If you have to either qualify or seek an exemption for the sale of some LLC interests, doing the same for all interests does not greatly add to your workload and should help ensure that you are in compliance with the securities laws, which is a good result. For contact information for the agency that administers securities in your state, see the appendix.

Converting a Sole Proprietorship to a Corporation

A sole proprietorship usually switches to a corporation in order to take advantage of one of the special characteristics unique to the corporate form, such as:

- **Corporate income and tax splitting.** Accumulated earnings and profits kept in the corporation are taxed at corporate tax rates of 15% and 25%, rates that are usually lower than the marginal (top) income tax rates of the individual business owners. If an owner keeps income in the business, it may make sense to incorporate so that the retained business earnings are taxed at lower corporate income tax rates.

- **Corporate access to private and public capital.** Incorporating allows you to issue standard (common) and special (preferred) shares—the usual diet for investment firms and public markets that invest in corporate stock in return for management, voting, and special dividend and liquidation rights.

- **Corporate equity-based employee plans.** The ability to create incentives for key employees with tax-favored employee stock options, restricted stock bonus and purchase plans, and other equity-based employee incentives is a unique, tax-favored benefit of the corporate form.

- **Built-in corporate structure.** If a sole proprietorship wants to step up to a larger business with separate management, supervisory, and investment roles, the standard corporate form automatically provides the framework. State corporation laws create separate director, officer, and shareholder positions, each with its own legal rights and responsibilities.

There may be other reasons for a sole proprietor to incorporate. For example, an unincorporated business owner may wish to incorporate to create special classes of stock in anticipation of handing over the reins of control and ownership to the next family generation, or in expectation of transferring closely held corporate stock to a publicly held acquiring corporation in a tax-free stock-swap deal. (For a discussion of tax-free corporate reorganizations, see Chapter 9.)

TIP

If you only want to limit personal liability, form an LLC. There are many good reasons to incorporate a sole proprietorship. However, if your sole aim is to avoid personal liability for business debts and claims, you'll probably be better off forming an LLC than a corporation. Forming an LLC allows you to achieve the legal advantage of limited liability protection while keeping your current pass-through tax status.

RESOURCE

Need help forming your corporation? For detailed information on forming a corporation, see *Incorporate Your Business: A Legal Guide to Forming a Corporation in Your State,* by Anthony Mancuso (Nolo). California incorporators can also use *How to Form Your Own California Corporation,* by Anthony Mancuso (Nolo).

Legal Procedures

A sole proprietor can incorporate alone or bring in additional owners at the time of incorporation. Typically, the sole proprietor transfers the assets and liabilities of the sole proprietorship to the corporation in return for shares, while any new co-owners pay cash or property into the corporation in exchange for their shares of stock. Here are the steps required to convert a sole proprietorship to a corporation:

- **File articles of incorporation.** The owner(s) must file articles of incorporation with the state filing office (typically, the corporations division of the secretary of state). All states allow a one-owner business to incorporate.

- **Choose directors and distribute shares.** If a corporation only has one owner (shareholder), it only has to have one director. Additional directors are required in some states if the corporation has more than one shareholder. In these states, if the corporation has two shareholders, at least two directors are required; if the corporation has three or more shareholders, at least three directors must be named. In some states, two separate individuals must fill specified officer positions—for example, a state may require the corporate president's position to be held by someone other than the corporate secretary. Information on corporate director and officer requirements can usually be found at the website for each state's business filing office. (See the appendix.)

- **Prepare corporate documentation.** The new owner(s) should prepare bylaws and issue stock certificates representing ownership interests in the corporation. Even a one-owner corporation should prepare this documentation, to show that the owner takes the legal existence of the corporation seriously. This will go a long way toward defeating efforts by your creditors or opponents in a lawsuit to "pierce the veil" of limited liability and go after your personal assets to satisfy your corporation's liabilities. (For more information, see "Piercing the Veil," in Chapter 2.)

- **Revise licenses, permits, and registrations.** The new corporate entity should obtain new permits, licenses, and registrations in the name of the corporation and cancel old licenses and permits taken out in the name of the now-defunct sole proprietorship. If the corporation will do business under a name different from the corporate name specified in its articles of incorporation, it should file a fictitious business name statement with the county clerk (or with the state corporations division in some states).

- **Get an EIN.** All corporations are required to obtain an employer identification number (EIN).

Income Tax Consequences of Conversion

Usually, you won't have to pay any taxes when you convert a sole proprietorship to a corporation. However, this tax-free treatment is not automatic. Section 351 of the Internal Revenue Code says that the incorporation is tax free only if the new shareholder (or shareholders, if new owners are admitted at the time of the incorporation) control the corporation immediately after the incorporation. Buying shareholders control the corporation if they own at least 80% of its shares. Most incorporations satisfy this control test; because they probably haven't issued stock before, there should be no existing shareholders to reduce the new buyers' control below the 80% control threshold.

> EXAMPLE: Cal, the sole owner of Cal's Construction, decides to incorporate to limit his personal liability from personal injuries that may occur on his construction sites. He transfers all assets and liabilities of the sole proprietorship to his new corporation, Cal's Construction Corp. (CCC), which his accountant values at a net asset (assets minus liabilities) figure of $500,000. CCC issues Cal 500,000 shares in the corporation for $1 per share. The incorporation should be tax-free to Cal under IRC Section 351.

As always, there are exceptions to these tax rules. For example, new shareholders will be taxed on the value of their stock if they receive shares in return for performing past or future services (the IRS views this as a taxable payment-for-services transaction). Also, if a shareholder receives property back from the corporation in addition to shares of stock, the shareholder must pay taxes on the fair market value of this extra property (property received by the shareholder other than shares of stock is called "boot" and is taxed by the IRS).

What if the incorporator transfers business assets to the new corporation in return for both shares of stock and a corporate promissory note in a part-equity, part-debt incorporation? The incorporator must pay taxes on the promissory note because it is treated as boot (property paid out to the incorporator by the corporation).

> **EXAMPLE:** Tom transfers the assets of his sole proprietorship, worth $100,000, to his new corporation for $25,000 in stock and a $75,000 corporate promissory note, obligating his corporation to make principal and interest payments to Tom in exchange for his transfer of $75,000 worth of assets to the corporation. The IRC 351 rules treat the principal of the note as income that is immediately taxable to the incorporator. Tom must pay taxes on the full $75,000 face value of the note, even though he will not receive the principal amount back until some time in the future. Tom will have to look to savings or sell other property to pay the taxes on this "boot income," which he has been allotted but has not received.

Another exception applies if the business liabilities transferred to (assumed by) the corporation exceed the owner's income tax basis in the transferred business assets. In that case, the business owner may owe income tax.

> **EXAMPLE:** Bob is a cash-basis sole proprietor—he reports income when he actually receives it and expenses when he actually pays them. Under standard tax rules, he has a zero basis in the accounts receivable of his

business (accounts receivable track money owed to the sole proprietorship by customers). If his only assets are these receivables and he transfers them along with $100,000 in liabilities to the corporation, the amount of transferred liabilities will exceed Bob's zero basis in business assets by $100,000. Bob will have to pay taxes on the $100,000 excess.

There are strategies that a tax specialist can devise to avoid this result—for example, the sole proprietor can lend money to the business prior to incorporation so that the basis in transferred assets exceeds the amount of liabilities. However, tax courts don't always approve these basis-increasing strategies. As always, you should get some expert help to assess and implement sophisticated tax savings.

 CAUTION

Avoid unexpected tax bills. IRC Section 351 is a minefield of tax traps, so have your tax adviser approve your incorporation plans before you file articles to convert an existing sole proprietorship into a corporation.

Tax Filing Procedures

Once you form a corporation, it is subject to the full corporate income tax regime contained in Subchapter C of Title 26 of the Internal Revenue Code. The business will have to pay corporate income tax (at corporate rates) on its profits and file a corporate income tax return, IRS Form 1120, *U.S. Corporation Income Tax Return*.

After converting to a corporation, a sole proprietor who works in the business becomes an employee of his or her corporation and will receive paychecks from it. Those checks will be subject to federal and state income tax withholding and other payroll deductions (FICA, FUTA, workers' compensation, state unemployment deductions, and the like).

The corporation must immediately begin withholding, depositing, reporting, and paying payroll taxes for the owner (and for any new owner who joins at the time of the incorporation and works for the corporation). This does not mean that you are going to pay more or less Social Security tax as a corporate employee than you did prior to incorporation. It simply means that your corporation will pay one-half of these taxes, and you, as a corporate employee, will pay the other half. In reality, both payments will come out of the same pocket (yours) before and after incorporation, so your total Social Security tax bill will be the same.

Complying with payroll procedures is a new experience for sole proprietors who did not have employees. The upside of this extra paperwork is that you no longer have to estimate and prepay income taxes quarterly. The corporation does the withholding for its employees, a category that includes officers, supervisors, staff, and anyone else who performs services for the corporation.

Paying Corporate Directors

The IRS makes an exception to corporate withholding requirements for paid directors. For example, directors may receive per-meeting payments or a flat annual fee for serving as a director. In the typical closely held corporation, the founders act as both directors and officers, and they are paid a salary only as corporate officers—that is, they serve on the board without pay.

If a corporation pays its directors for serving, the director, not the corporation, is responsible for reporting and paying tax on the payments. Specifically, the director must report these payments as self-employment income on the director's annual income tax return and pay both income tax and self-employment tax on the payments.

> **TIP**
>
> **Get your finances in order.** A new corporate business should establish an orderly double-entry bookkeeping system. Expect to hand over your double-entry financial books to a tax specialist at the end of the year, so he or she can prepare your annual corporate income tax returns.

S Corporation Tax Election Procedures

As explained in Chapter 1, an S corporation qualifies for special tax treatment under the Internal Revenue Code (and state corporate tax statutes as well). Electing S corporation tax status puts the owner more or less back in the tax position of a sole proprietor.

To make the Subchapter S election, the corporation files IRS Form 2553, *Election by a Small Business Corporation*. Once the election is filed, the corporation's profits, losses, deductions, credits, and other tax items pass through to the owner.

> **TIP**
>
> **Consider forming an LLC instead.** For a variety of reasons (covered in more detail in Chapter 1), it's often more advantageous for a business owner to simply form an LLC than to incorporate and seek S corporation status to be taxed as a pass-through entity.

Although S corporation rules are more complex than the basic sole proprietor rules, the owner of the S corporation will have business profits pass through to him or her at the end of the tax year, similar to the pass-through of business profits when the business was operated as a sole proprietorship. This also means that an S corporation owner can be taxed on business profits earned each year—even if these profits are not actually paid out to the owners.

CAUTION

S corporation employees may not be eligible for fringe benefits.
Once a corporation elects S corporation tax status, any shareholder-
employee who owns more than 2% of the S corporation stock is not eligible
to deduct certain corporate employee fringe benefits, such as $50,000 worth
of group term-life insurance premiums or medical reimbursement payments.
For more information on S corporations, see Chapter 1.

Self-Employment Taxes

Once a sole proprietorship is incorporated, the corporation pays half
of the Social Security tax owed on the owner-employee's wages; the
owner-employee pays the other half (via a payroll deduction from his or
her corporate salary). Because corporate profits are the owner's profits,
however, the sole owner is really paying the full Social Security tax, just
as he or she did before incorporation—the money is just coming out of
two separate bank accounts.

TIP

Special Social Security tax rule for S corporations. Profits passed
through an S corporation and allocated to its owner are not subject to self-
employment tax. Some S corporation owners take advantage of this rule
by reducing their S corporation salary and instead getting paid directly out
of the profits of the S corporation. Unlike a regular C corporation, these
S corporation profits are taxed just once to the S corporation shareholder—
and not to the corporation at corporate tax rates. Although this rule might
make S corporation tax status seem attractive to a sole proprietor who is
converting to a corporation, it's not necessarily the best strategy, particularly
because it will lower the Social Security credits of the owner-employee (and,
therefore, the amount to be paid out when the employee becomes eligible
to receive benefits). If you are considering electing S corporation status to
reduce your self-employment taxes, consult your financial adviser first.

Securities Laws Procedures

A share of stock in a corporation is a "security," plain and simple. When you convert a sole proprietorship to a corporation, you will be selling yourself a security that you must either register under federal or state securities laws or qualify for an exemption from these laws.

The purpose of securities law protections and disclosures is to protect the buyer from fraudulent or unscrupulous sellers of securities. Because you are selling shares to yourself when you incorporate a sole proprietorship, this consumer fraud shield has no real-life applicability to your situation. Nonetheless, it's usually easy enough to demonstrate that your incorporation and sale of stock meet the technical legal requirements and qualify for an exemption from the securities laws. It's a good idea to do so, just to show that you are treating your new corporation as a separate legal entity and following all the legal rules.

If you bring additional owners into your corporation when you incorporate your sole proprietorship, complying with securities laws protects the interests of your co-owners. After all, the new owners will be investing in a business that you have operated alone for some period of time, and you will want to make sure they understand both its financial history and its reasonably predictable future by making the disclosures required by the securities rules.

Federal and state securities law exemptions often allow you to form a small, privately held corporation with no (or minimal) security law filings and paperwork, as long as you only sell shares privately, without advertising, to:

- people who will be active in running the corporation (such as directors and officers), or

- a small number of sophisticated investors who have sufficient experience in financial matters to protect their own interests.

You can find information on how to contact your state securities law office in the appendix. ●

Converting a Partnership to Another Entity

W hen Steve Wozniak and Steve Jobs brought their first Apple 1 computer to the Homebrew Computer Club in Palo Alto in April 1976, few people took them—or their computer— seriously. Once the two partners started taking orders, however, their low-cost ($666.66) microcomputer system slowly began to sell. Within nine months, Jobs and Wozniak filed incorporation documents and, on January 3, 1977, converted their partnership to a corporation.

The migration Wozniak and Jobs made from partnership to corporation was typical of many successful business entities in the 1970s and later decades. Today, many successful partnerships decide to form LLCs rather than corporations, to help the owners avoid personal legal liability for business debts and claims while maintaining their pass-through tax status. This chapter examines how a partnership can convert to a different legal entity—and the paperwork, tax, and security law implications associated with each conversion.

Converting a Partnership to a Sole Proprietorship

Any time a partnership dwindles down to one owner—for example, because one partner in a two-partner business dies or buys out the other—the partnership automatically dissolves and becomes a sole proprietorship.

Legal Procedures

You won't have to file formal paperwork with the state to change your general partnership to a sole proprietorship.

> **CAUTION**
>
> **Limited partnerships may have to file papers with the state.** If you are dissolving a limited partnership, you will have to submit paperwork to the state's filing office to legally terminate the partnership.

The new sole proprietor should take the following steps:

- **Review the termination provisions of the partnership agreement.** If the former partnership had a partnership agreement, you will need to follow the termination provisions established in the agreement. For example, the agreement may provide for liquidation rights between the owners and spell out the post-termination rights and responsibilities regarding ownership of the business name or other partnership assets.

- **Revise licenses, permits, and registrations.** The new sole proprietor should cancel any licenses, permits, and registrations issued in the name of the partnership, then take out new permits and licenses in the name of the new sole proprietorship. If the sole proprietorship will operate under a name other than that of the owner, a new fictitious business name registration should also be filed. Some states require the business to file a notice of dissolution of partnership in a newspaper—any newspaper that handles legal notices can tell you how to accomplish this routine filing.

- **Get an EIN.** A sole proprietorship who will maintain a retirement plan (such as a Keogh plan) or hire employees should obtain an EIN and use it when reporting and paying employment taxes and making retirement plan filings and contributions. Note: Anyone who receives a salary (including a sole proprietor's spouse who works in the business) is an employee on whose behalf payroll taxes must be withheld and paid to the IRS and state. A sole owner who will not maintain a retirement plan or hire employees can use his or her Social Security number when completing Schedule C, *Profits and Loss From Business*, filed with the owner's annual 1040 income tax return.

- **File notice of dissolution of partnership with county clerk or recorder.** In many states, a dissolving general or limited partnership must make a local filing with the county clerk or county recorder. This minor formality is intended to let creditors of the partnership and others know when it is going out of business or changing its form. To find out if this is required in your jurisdiction, call a local newspaper that handles legal filings and ask if they publish a notice of dissolution of partnership or similar form required in your state. If they do, ask them to send you one to fill out, then have them publish it.

Income Tax Consequences of Conversion

The dissolution of a partnership is a taxable exchange of assets from the partnership to the former partners. This dissolution/conversion can result in taxable gain and income to the ex-partners, even though one of the owners stays in business as a sole proprietor.

The 50% Rule

There's a special tax rule that affects partnerships (and co-owned LLCs, which are treated like partnerships for tax purposes) in which 50% or more of the business's capital and profits interests change hands during a 12-month period. This rule applies not only to the conversion of a partnership to a sole proprietorship, but also to any other transfer of partnership (or LLC) ownership interests in which 50% or more of the interests in the business changes hands

Section 708 of the Internal Revenue Code treats the transfer of 50% or more of the interests in a partnership (or LLC) as a tax termination of a partnership. In other words, the tax code treats the transfer of 50% or more of interests as though the business had dissolved, even if it stays in business and continues to have two or more owners and even if the interests are sold or exchanged between owners.

Therefore, whenever (1) a partnership (or LLC) is converted into a sole proprietorship, (2) 50% or more of the partnership's (or LLC's) interests are sold or transferred, or (3) the partnership (or LLC) is formally dissolved, each owner may owe taxes. All current and former owners should consult with their tax advisers to understand the income tax consequences.

Tax Filing Procedures

After a partnership changes to a sole proprietorship, the remaining sole owner reports profits and losses on his or her 1040 Schedule C, *Profit or Loss from Business*. The partnership should file a final Form 1065, *U.S. Return of Partnership Income,* and prepare final K-1s (*Partner's Share of Income, Deductions, Credits, etc.*) for each of the former partners. For more information on partnership tax reporting, see Chapter 4.

Self-Employment Tax Status of Owners

Converting a partnership to a sole proprietorship does not change the self-employment tax treatment of the owner who remains active in the business. Sole proprietors, like the partners of a general partnership and managing partners of a limited partnership, must pay self-employment taxes on business profits.

Securities Laws Procedures

The conversion of a partnership to a sole proprietorship generally won't involve security law procedures or concerns, because the sale of business interests to a sole proprietor doesn't qualify as the sale of a security under state and federal securities laws.

> **CAUTION**
>
> **Dissolving a limited partnership is more complicated.** If you are dissolving a limited partnership and cashing out a limited partner, you are, in effect, buying back a security interest, because a limited partnership interest is considered a security. In a worst-case scenario, a limited partner who feels that a buy-back or cash-out did not abide by the terms of the limited partnership agreement or the partner's reasonable expectations of a return on his or her prior investment in the partnership may make a securities law fraud claim at the state or federal level. Because of this possibility, you may wish to consult with an attorney when dissolving a limited partnership.

Converting a Partnership to an LLC

Many partnerships decide to convert to LLCs. Typically, the partners do this to obtain limited liability protection for their personal assets.

Both general and limited partnerships can be converted to LLCs. General partners in either type of partnership get limited liability protection once the LLC is formed. If a limited partnership is converted to an LLC, not only do the prior limited partners maintain their limited liability protection, but they are also allowed to participate in LLC management.

A general partnership can convert to an LLC in most states with a modest amount of paperwork and fees, and with no change to income tax treatment and filing requirements. Of course, as with all legal and tax rules, there are exceptions and strategies that may affect a partnership's conversion to an LLC.

Partnership-to-LLC: Reassessing Commitments

A partnership may convert to an LLC during a "growth spurt" in the life of the business. This can be an ideal time for each partner to reassess his or her commitment to the business, and some partners may decide to cash out their interests and let the other owners move forward into the next stage. If the business cannot afford to buy out a departing partner, the partner who wants to step aside from an active role in the business can continue as an owner, but with a redefined role in the business. The various LLC management structures let owners redefine their role and stay in the business on their own terms—as managers, investors, or both.

Legal Procedures

This section analyzes the legal procedures required for converting a general or limited partnership to an LLC.

General Partnerships

To change a general partnership to an LLC, the partners must take the following actions:

- **Agree to terminate the partnership and convert to an LLC.** Most partnership agreements require the unanimous consent of all partners to dissolve or change the form of the business. Even if your agreement doesn't require this, it's probably best to get everyone on board by obtaining unanimous approval. (You don't want to drag a reluctant partner into your new LLC.) You may have to complete additional paperwork to legally terminate your partnership when you convert it to an LLC. Your state may require you to publish a notice of dissolution of partnership in a newspaper of general circulation in the county where the principal office of the partnership was located—a routine filing that most newspapers are set up to handle for a modest fee. Call the legal notice department of your local newspapers to find out whether this procedure is required in your state and, if so, how much you have to pay to publish this notice.

- **File articles of organization.** The owner(s) must file LLC articles of organization with the state filing office (typically, the corporations division of the secretary of state's office). Many states provide an online articles form specifically for partnerships converting to LLCs.

EXAMPLE: Rachid and Chi-Yuan want to convert their electronics consulting partnership, Silikonics, to an LLC. Silikonics is a general partnership, and each owner is a 50% partner. They look at the official LLC forms list on their state's filing office website and notice a standard articles of organization form but no separate form specifically for converting a partnership to an LLC (often called an articles of conversion form). Rachid downloads the standard articles form and fills it in, the two partners sign as LLC organizers (only one signature is required, but they want to sign the form together to show that they both agreed to the conversion), and then Rachid mails it to the state for filing along with a check for the required articles filing fee. Rachid calls a local newspaper and asks if it has a notice of dissolution of partnership publication. The newspaper does, so Rachid provides the information and pays the fee by phone, and the newspaper makes the require publication. At the end of the notice publication period (in this state, three successive publications one week apart are required), the newspaper sends Rachid an affidavit of publication with copies of the newspaper publication clippings. Rachid places these papers in the LLC records book to keep a paper trail of the conversion process.

- **Prepare operating agreement.** The new owners should create an LLC operating agreement documenting ownership interests, profits, losses, voting and liquidation rights, and the other rights and responsibilities of the members. The operating agreement should indicate how the LLC will be managed—either by all members (owners), which is called member-management, or by a select management team (who may be members or nonmembers), which is called manager-management. (For a more detailed explanation of LLC management structures, see "Partnership to LLC: The Freedom *Not* to Manage," below.) Typically, when a general partnership is converted to an LLC, the LLC owners choose member-management, because this structure replicates the way general partnerships are managed. Normally the capital, profits, and voting interests of the prior partners as specified in the partnership agreement are carried over to the LLC operating agreement. Although the LLC operating agreement will contain many of the same provisions found in the partnership agreement, some fine-tuning may be appropriate to reflect the nuances of

LLC tax treatment (see "Partnership to LLC: The Freedom *Not* to Manage" and "Get Tax Advice When Fine-Tuning Your Operating Agreement," below). This is true even though co-owned LLCs generally are treated like partnerships under federal and state law.

Partnership to LLC: The Freedom *Not* to Manage

If all of the owners of a prior partnership want to continue to manage the business, the LLC should adopt a member-management structure in the operating agreement. This makes each member (owner) a managing member who can vote on management decisions and act as an agent of the LLC (that is, he or she can speak for the business to the outside world and bind the LLC to contracts and other business deals).

If any of the partners have decided that they don't want an active role in the business—but still want a share of the profits—that's fine, too. The LLC is an ideal vehicle to let prior partners transition to a new role in the business. In that case, the LLC can adopt a manager-managed structure, and the partner who wishes to step to the sidelines can become a nonmanaging member in the new LLC. A nonmanaging member doesn't get to vote on management issues nor act as agent for the LLC but continues to get distributive shares of the LLC's profits according to the terms specified in the LLC operating agreement.

- **Revise licenses, permits, and registrations.** The new entity should obtain new permits, licenses, and registrations in the name of the LLC and cancel old licenses and permits taken out in the name of the now-defunct partnership. If the LLC will do business under a name different from the LLC name specified in its articles of organization, it should file a fictitious business name statement with the county clerk.

• **Get an EIN.** Because the LLC will be treated as a partnership, it must obtain an employer identification number (EIN) to prepare its annual IRS and state information returns. An EIN is required even if the co-owned LLC has no employees and the LLC and owners do not set up retirement plans. If the prior partnership had an EIN, the LLC can continue to use that number.

Get Tax Advice When Fine-Tuning Your Operating Agreement

When you convert a partnership agreement to an LLC operating agreement, it's best not to simply transfer each provision verbatim. This can backfire if, for example, the partnership agreement gave partners a percentage of the profits (or losses) that does not correspond to the percentage of each partner's capital contribution. In this case, the partnership agreement probably contained special provisions to ensure that the IRS and state would accept these "special allocations" of profits and losses. Often, one of these provisions provides for what's known as "negative capital account restoration," which provides for a method of "making up" these deficiencies when the partnership is dissolved.

If this type of provision is carried over to the LLC operating agreement, an LLC member with a negative capital account balance will have to personally pay money back into the LLC when he or she leaves the business. Because the whole point of forming an LLC is to avoid this sort of personal liability for business operations, you will want to ask your tax adviser to help you structure the LLC to avoid this result (the IRC regulations provide another way to set up special allocations in an operating agreement without forcing LLC members to restore negative account balances).

There are other special tax provisions in many LLC operating agreements that may require some fine-tuning when you convert a partnership to an LLC. Consult with a tax adviser when you're ready to fine-tune your LLC operating agreement.

Limited Partnerships

In order to change a limited partnership to an LLC, the partners must:

• **Agree to terminate the limited partnership and convert to an LLC.** Just like a general partnership, a limited partnership must agree to dissolve and convert to an LLC. However, unlike a general partnership, a limited partnership is commonly (and officially) dissolved by filing documentation with the state office that handles corporate, partnership, and LLC paperwork (often the corporations division of the secretary of state's office). If your state uses an articles of conversion form (see "Articles of Conversion: A Direct Route to Limited Liability," below), this document will accomplish the task. If your state does not provide a special articles of conversion form that expressly says you are converting your existing limited partnership to an LLC, you will probably need to file a certificate of cancellation of limited partnership. The best way to find the necessary requirements and forms is to browse your state's entity filing office website (see the links in the appendix). In either case—whether you file a certificate of cancellation or articles of conversion—you may still need to publish a notice of dissolution of limited partnership in a newspaper of general circulation in the county where the principal office of the partnership was located. Call the legal notice department of your local newspapers to find out whether this procedure is required in your state.

• **File articles of organization.** The owners of the limited partnership must file LLC articles of organization with the state filing office (typically, the corporations division of the secretary of state's office). Many states provide an online LLC articles form specifically designed to handle the conversion of a partnership to an LLC. As stated above, if you use this special articles of conversion form to convert a limited partnership to an LLC, you probably do not also have to file a certificate of cancellation of limited partnership.

EXAMPLE: Let's assume that Silikonics from the previous example is a limited partnership. Because the state does not provide a special articles of conversion of partnership to LLC form on its filing office website, Rachid prepares and files standard articles of organization as in the previous example. He then downloads a certificate of cancellation of limited partnership form from the state website, fills it in, and files it, showing the date when the LLC articles were filed as the effective date of the cancellation of the certificate of limited partnership. If Rachid had found an articles of conversion of partnership to LLC form on the state website, he would prepare and file this form to both create the LLC and cancel the certificate of limited partnership. He would not have to separately file a cancellation of certificate of limited partnership form.

- **Prepare operating agreement.** The new owners should create an LLC operating agreement documenting ownership interests, profits, losses, voting and liquidation rights, and the other rights and responsibilities of the members. Typically, when a limited partnership is converted to an LLC, the LLC owners choose manager-management, because this structure replicates the way a limited partnership is managed. The former general partner(s) acts as the new manager-member of the LLC, and the prior limited partners become nonmanaging members. Similarly, the capital, profits, and voting interests of the prior partners as specified in the partnership agreement are carried over to the LLC operating agreement. As noted, some fine-tuning of the LLC operating agreement may be appropriate. (See "Get Tax Advice When Fine-Tuning Your Operating Agreement," above).

- **Revise licenses, permits, and registrations.** The new entity should obtain new permits, licenses, and registrations in the name of the LLC and cancel old licenses and permits taken out in the name of the now-defunct partnership. If the LLC will do business under a name different from the LLC name specified in its articles of organization, it should file a fictitious business name statement with the county clerk.

- **Continue to use EIN.** An LLC converted from an existing limited partnership can continue to use the EIN of the prior limited partnership.

Income Tax Consequences of Conversion

Generally, there are no immediate income tax consequences when a partnership converts to an LLC. The conversion is usually not considered a taxable sale or exchange under federal and state tax law, provided that:

- Business operations are continued after the conversion.
- The owners keep the same capital, profits, loss, and liability sharing ratios in the LLC that they had in the prior partnership.

For example, if two equal partners each keep a 50% profit, loss, and capital interest in the new LLC and continue to share liabilities 50/50 after the conversion, the conversion is a tax-free transaction.

RESOURCE

How to research IRS tax rulings on partnership-LLC conversions. To research IRS tax rulings on partnership-LLC conversions, go to Legal Bitstream (www.legalbitstream.com) and click "Revenue Rulings," on the left side of the home page. Then search for Revenue Rulings 84-52 and 95-37 (for example, type "Revenue Ruling 84-52" in the search box). These are the primary IRS pronouncements on how conversions are treated.

If you change the owners' capital, profits, loss, or liability sharing ratios at the time of the conversion, the transaction may be taxable to one or more of the prior partners. This follows from the 50% rule, discussed earlier for partnerships, which also applies to LLCs. (See "The 50% Rule," above.)

Here are a few sample scenarios of partnership-to-LLC conversions that can trigger tax consequences.

EXAMPLE 1: Rachid, Chi-Yuan, and Hari want to convert their electronics integrated circuit design consulting partnership, Silikonics, to an LLC. Silikonics is a general partnership, and each partner owns a third of the business. Hari has had enough of the stress of managing the business and worrying about quarterly profits. He wants to hand over the reins to the other partners and change his status to a salaried employee. He will probably make less money in the long term, but at least he will be guaranteed a regular salary payment as long as the business stays successful. He sells his one-third interest to the other partners, who buy Hari out under the buy-out terms specified in their partnership agreement. The two-owner Silikonics partnership is converted to a two-owner LLC, and Hari is hired as an LLC employee.

Before making the switch to a two-member LLC, the partners checked with their tax adviser. They were told that a sale of a one-third interest would not trigger a tax termination of the partnership, a result the partners wanted to avoid because it could mean that the partners would owe tax on the sale. If Hari had owned 50% or more of the capital and profits interests of the partnership, selling his interests—even to the other partners—would have triggered a tax termination of the partnership under Section 708 of the Internal Revenue Code, as explained in "The 50% Rule," above. Because Hari has sold his partnership interest, his sale is a taxable transaction, and he will have to pay tax on the sale if he realizes a gain (that is, if the proceeds of the sale exceed Hari's income tax basis in his partnership interest).

The tax adviser also feels that the sale of Hari's interest followed by a later conversion of the two-partner firm to a two-member LLC will not be treated by the IRS as a single transaction. If it was, it could mean that a three-member partnership was converted to a two-member LLC, and this shifting of interests at the time of a conversion may not be tax-free to Rachid and Chi-Yuan. (A conversion is generally tax-free only if the existing partners have the same interests in the LLC that they had in the preexisting partnership.)

EXAMPLE 2: Neither Silikonics, the partnership, nor Rachid and Chi-Yuan personally can afford to buy out Hari's interest, nor can they locate a lender willing to advance the funds necessary to buy out Hari's partnership share. Instead, Rachid and Chi-Yuan suggest that Hari stay on as a nonmanaging member of the LLC and a salaried employee. He will receive a lower capital and profits interest in the LLC (relative to his prior partnership percentages) because he is now a nonmanaging member, and he will be paid a salary for future work for the LLC. Hari agrees and the three move on to the next incarnation of the business as an LLC.

Because each partner is changing his ownership interests, each knows it is important to check with a tax adviser to find out whether anyone will owe taxes because of the conversion. The partners also have the partnership's tax adviser look over the conversion plan and suggest changes that may be necessary to make the partnership agreement work as their new LLC operating agreement.

CAUTION

A potential tax trap exists when you convert a partnership to an LLC. Partnerships and LLCs allocate liabilities differently. In a partnership, general partners are personally liable for repayment of partnership debts. In an LLC, no owner of the LLC is personally on the hook for the LLC's liabilities. The IRS has established rules regarding the tax treatment of LLC members when partnership debts are assumed by the new LLC. These rules are fairly complex, but the main point is this: Converting a partnership to an LLC can result in tax liability for one or more of the prior partners if they are relieved of personal liability for a partnership debt that is assumed by the LLC. You can review these rules by viewing Publication 541, *Partnerships* (see the section called *Terminating a Partnership*), at the IRS website (www.irs.gov). These rules are remarkably complicated, even by IRS standards, so before you decide to convert, you should seek the advice of a tax consultant about the possible tax consequences of having your new LLC assume the debts of your prior partnership.

Tax Filing Procedures

After a partnership is converted to a co-owned LLC, the LLC continues to file a partnership tax return, IRS Form 1065, *U.S. Return of Partnership Income,* at the end of each tax year (there are no special LLC federal tax forms; LLCs use federal partnership tax forms). The LLC also continues to prepare a 1065 Schedule K-1, *Partner's Share of Income, Deductions, Credits, etc.,* for each LLC member. The K-1 shows the amount of LLC income or loss, deductions, and credits each LLC member must report on his or her individual 1040 tax return. The basic income tax treatment of profits earned in the business remains the same after the conversion of a partnership to an LLC. LLC members, like partners, report and pay income tax on all profits earned each year in the business, whether or not the profits are actually paid out in cash by the business to the members.

LLC members are not considered employees for payroll tax purposes.

EXAMPLE: Adelle and Vance are equal owners of Advance Lending, LLC. Both contributed equally to start the company, and each has a 50% capital, profits, and voting interest in the LLC. However, Vance also works for the LLC full time in the company's office. The firm pays Vance $100,000 annually for this work. This year, the LLC's net profits, after deducting Vance's salary plus other operating expenses, are $250,000. The LLC does not withhold or pay payroll tax on Vance's $100,000 salary nor on the $250,000 profits allocated to Adelle and Vance, but each owner must report, estimate, and pay individual income tax on the $125,000 of LLC profits allocated to each owner (even if the allocated profits are not actually paid out to the owners). Vance must also estimate and pay income and self employment taxes on his $100,000 salary.

Self-Employment Tax Status of Owners

LLC owners must pay self-employment taxes only on profits allocated to owners who are active in the business and on other types of payments made to owners, such as earned income paid to owners for working for the LLC. Converting a partnership to an LLC generally does not change the self-employment tax status of the business owners as long as they don't change their active or inactive status in the business. For example, if the general partners of the prior partnership are selected as the managing members of the LLC (as is typical), profits allocated to the managing LLC members will continue to be subject to self-employment tax. And, if a limited partnership is converted to an LLC and the limited partners become nonmanaging LLC members, profits allocated to the nonmanaging owners should continue to be exempt from self-employment tax.

There is one important caveat, however. This analysis is based on some guesswork as to how the current self-employment tax rules apply to LLCs. To get up-to-date answers for LLC self-employment tax questions, ask your tax adviser.

> **CAUTION**
> **An owner of an LLC is not an employee.** For payroll tax purposes, an LLC owner is not considered an employee, so profits allocated to an owner are not subject to payroll taxes. The owner must estimate and pay income tax on these allocated profits as well as on any other income paid to the owner (for example, income paid in return for services).

Securities Laws Procedures

As long as each LLC member is active in the business (as is the case in a member-managed LLC), the owner's new interest in the LLC should not be considered a security under federal and state securities laws.

(Remember, a "security" is defined as the sale of an interest with the expectation of earning profits from the efforts of others.)

However, the following conversion scenarios may create a security interest subject to state and federal securities rules:

- In a member-managed LLC, if new owners come on board who will not be active in the business and have no voting rights or are otherwise kept out of the decision-making loop, issuing LLC membership interests to these passive investors most likely will be subject to federal and state securities laws.

- If the partners create a manager-managed LLC, the sale of LLC interests probably will be considered a sale of securities under the federal and state rules. The nonmanaging members, who legally are not granted management rights, are investing with the expectation of earning profits from the efforts of others (the managing-members)—this is a classic example of a "security."

 RELATED TOPIC

You can find information on how to contact your state securities law office in the appendix.

CAUTION

Some states take an all-or-nothing approach to LLC securities regulation. Some states categorically state that unless all members manage your LLC, you must treat all sales of LLC interests, even sales to managing members, as "securities." This means that you must qualify or seek an exemption for the sale of all LLC interests. For contact information for the agency that administers securities in your state, see the appendix.

Converting a Partnership to a Corporation

Before LLCs appeared on the legal scene, partners had to convert to a corporation to obtain legal liability protection for all owners. Now that LLCs can be formed in any state, most partnerships that want legal liability protection plus pass-through tax status will convert the partnership to an LLC, not a corporation.

There still are several reasons for business owners to consider converting their business to a corporation, however.

Reasons to Incorporate Your Partnership

Here are some reasons why you may choose to convert your partnership to a corporation rather than an LLC.

Attracting Capital

The most common reason why partnerships incorporate is to attract additional sources of capital. Private venture capital companies typically fund only corporations, because only the corporate form can satisfy their need for special management, dividend, liquidation, and voting rights that attach to special classes of preferred corporate stock. Sophisticated investors and venture fund managers know that investing in a corporation provides the best exit strategy for cashing out their investment in a business. Below is a typical example of how a partnership may convert its assets for the benefit of a newly funded corporation.

EXAMPLE: Gina and Celine, programmers and business partners, created the video adventure game *Galacticants*, which features acid-spewing cyber ants roaming the galaxy, plundering planets, and making slaves of captured insect populations. Adelle and Vance, the owners of Advance Lending, LLC (in the prior example) have lunch with Gina and Celine and express their interest in funding a start-up company organized as a corporation to develop and license the game. Adelle and Vance are willing to invest cash to rent office space and hire an experienced software management and development team to complete a professional grade prototype to pitch the game to video game companies. In return, Gina and Vance will be asked to transfer their partnership assets—the software code and their rights in the software—to the new corporation for shares of stock.

Advance Lending will be a 52% common shareholder, and Gina and Vance will each be 24% common shareholders. Advance Lending also will get an additional 10% of the total number of common shares in nonvoting preferred shares that have a special right to dividends (assuming earnings and profits of the corporation meet a specified threshold). In addition, Advanced Lending will be guaranteed a return of five times the original cost of the preferred shares before any sales proceeds are paid out on the common shares. One of the two partners, Gina or Celine, will serve on the corporation's three-person board of directors along with Adelle and Vance, so Advance Lending will hold a two-thirds majority on the board and control the management of the corporation.

Gina and Celine agree to check with their legal and tax advisers and then get back to Adelle and Vance about converting their partnership to a corporation under the proposed terms.

Cumulative Voting

Another unique characteristic of a corporation is cumulative voting—a process that gives minority shareholders in a corporation a bit of extra clout when electing candidates to the board of directors. Here's an example of how cumulative voting procedures work.

EXAMPLE: Gina and Celine, from the previous example, decide to create a corporation with the aid and funding of Advance Lending. Advance Lending will be a 52% common shareholder, and Gina and Vance will each be 24% common shareholders. Under normal corporate shareholder voting rules, each shareholder has a right to cast all of his or her votes on each matter submitted to shareholders for a vote. Because Advance Lending holds a majority of the common voting shares, it can vote all 52 shares for each candidate to the board and, therefore, can effectively decide who will hold each of the three seats.

However, under cumulative voting, each board member gets total votes equal to the member's shares, multiplied by the number of directors to be elected, and the candidates with the highest number of votes get elected to the board (up to the number of board members to be elected). In other words, if three board seats are to be filled, the three candidates with the most votes get elected to the board for another term. Under cumulative voting, Advance Lending will have a total of 156 votes (52×3) to cast for all candidates, while Gina and Celine will have 72 (24×3) total votes each. Advance will want to cast at least 73 votes for Adelle and 73 votes for Vance to reelect them to the board at each annual meeting of shareholders. Advance will not want to vote 72 or less for any candidate, because either Gina or Celine has sufficient votes to tie or beat a vote of 72 votes for a candidate. In short, cumulative voting procedures ensure that Gina and Celine have sufficient votes to elect the third candidate. They probably will want to agree each year to pool their votes (144 combined votes) to reelect either one or the other of the pair to the third board seat. If they do not pool their votes (for example, each votes 72 votes for herself), a tie vote for the third board seat would force a runoff election. Because Advance Lending is entitled to vote its total 156 shares at the runoff election, it could determine who held the third board seat—a result that defeats the cumulative voting advantage to Gina and Celine.

Other Corporate Advantages

There are additional reasons why partnerships seeking liability protection choose a corporation rather than an LLC:

- **Corporate income and tax splitting.** If an owner keeps income in the business, it may make sense to incorporate so that the retained business earnings are taxed at lower corporate income tax rates. Accumulated earnings and profits kept in the corporation are taxed at corporate tax rates of 15% and 25%, which are usually lower than the marginal (top) income tax rates of the individual business owners.

- **Corporate equity-based employee plans.** Corporations can create incentives for owner-employees and other key employees through tax-favored employee stock options, restricted stock bonus and purchase plans, and other equity-based employee incentives. These options are not available to LLCs.

- **Built-in corporate structure with statutory framework.** The standard corporate form automatically provides the framework—through separate director, officer, and shareholder positions, each with separate legal rights and responsibilities—for a partnership to step up to a business with separate management, supervisory, and investment tiers.

- **Corporate tax-free perks.** Corporations can offer special tax-free perks to employees—for example, a corporate employee does not have to report and pay individual income tax on amounts paid as part of a qualified medical reimbursement plan or on premiums paid for up to $50,000 worth of qualified term-life insurance. If you work in your business, you automatically become its employee when you incorporate. This means that you, as an employee in your corporation, can receive these tax-free perks along with other corporate employees.

There are other advantages written into the Internal Revenue Code that sometimes tip the scales in favor of converting to a corporation rather than an LLC. For example, corporations can issue tax-favored ISOs (incentive stock options) to employees or participate in a tax-free corporate reorganization, where an acquiring corporation buys another in a stock swap. The special tax perks that go along with the corporate form are of particular interest to entrepreneurs that have their sights set on forming, growing, or being acquired by a larger business. If you want to start more modestly, it probably makes sense to convert your partnership to an LLC, then wait for a while before deciding whether to take the next growth step of converting to a corporation. (For a discussion of converting an LLC to a corporation, see Chapter 8.)

CAUTION

Incorporating is usually a one-way street. Once you incorporate, converting the corporation to another type of legal business entity is typically a taxable event, which can trigger a substantial tax liability for both the corporation and its shareholders. In other words, unlike converting a sole proprietorship, partnership, or LLC to a corporation, converting a corporation to a sole proprietorship, partnership, or LLC means that the corporation is dissolved for both legal and tax purposes, and both the corporation and its shareholders may have to pay income taxes.

Once you form a regular C corporation, you aren't stuck with it until the corporation goes out of business or is sold, however. A C corporation can elect S corporation tax treatment to achieve a modified form of pass-through taxation for the business and its owners, and later change back to C corporation tax status, without triggering taxes based on the conversion (with some exceptions, of course). For information on switching a C corporation to an S corporation, see Chapter 9.

A privately held corporation can (with expert tax help) convert to another corporation tax-free, typically when it is sold in a tax-free corporate reorganization in which a privately held corporation is bought out by a publicly held buying corporation. For more information on the basic tax treatment of corporate reorganizations, see Chapter 9.

Legal Procedures

In order to change a general partnership to a corporation, the partners
must take the following actions:

- **Agree to terminate the partnership and convert to a corporation.**
  Most partnership agreements require the unanimous consent of all
  partners to dissolve or change the form of the business. Even if your
  agreement doesn't impose this requirement, it's probably best to
  get everyone on board by obtaining unanimous approval. After all,
  incorporating will change the tax and legal status of the partners,
  so each partner should approve the change. You may have to file
  additional paperwork to legally terminate a partnership when you
  convert it to a corporation. Your state may require you to publish
  a notice of dissolution of partnership in a newspaper of general
  circulation in the county where the principal office of the partnership
  was located—a routine filing that most newspapers are set up to
  handle for a modest fee. Call the legal notice department of your
  local newspapers to find out whether this procedure is required in
  your state and, if so, how much you have to pay to publish this
  notice.

- **File articles of incorporation.** The owner(s) must prepare and file
  articles of incorporation with the state corporate filing office. Standard
  articles forms are available online at state corporate filing office
  websites. (See the appendix.) Articles must be accompanied by
  the required filing fee, which typically is a flat fee or is based on the
  number and type of shares authorized in the articles. In many states,
  you can terminate a general or limited partnership and convert it
  to a corporation by filing articles of conversion. (See "Articles of
  Conversion: A Direct Route to Limited Liability," below.) If your
  state does not provide a conversion form or you simply prefer not to
  prepare one, you can convert your partnership to a corporation by
  making any required filing to dissolve your partnership, as explained

above, preparing and filing standard articles of incorporation, then transferring the assets and liabilities of the prior partnership over to your new corporation. You can document this transfer by preparing a standard bill of sale. Always check with your tax adviser before deciding how to convert to a corporation, since different types of conversions can have different tax consequences.

- **Transfer assets and liabilities; issue shares.** Typically, the former partners transfer the assets and liabilities of the partnership to the new corporation in return for shares of stock. Partners usually receive a percentage of shares in the corporation in a proportion that is equal to their share in the assets of the prior partnership. If any new co-owners (such as passive investors) are brought into the new corporation, they pay in additional cash or property for their shares of stock.

CAUTION

To convert a limited partnership to a corporation, you must file paperwork with the state to terminate the partnership. Typically, this form is called a certificate of cancellation of limited partnership, which must be signed by all of the general partners of the LP. You can find a standard downloadable form on most state corporate filing office websites. (See the appendix for links to your state's corporate filing website.)

Articles of Conversion: A Direct Route to Limited Liability

Some states allow a general or limited partnership (or LLC) to convert to a corporation by filing special articles of conversion. You don't have to use articles of conversion, but it makes the conversion process a little easier. In states that allow this filing, a form may be available on the state's corporate filing office website. If not, the form must be prepared by the incorporators (or their lawyers), who must draft it according to the requirements listed in the state's corporation law.

If you prepare and file articles of conversion to convert the prior partnership (or LLC) to a corporation, no other form is required to terminate the prior partnership (or LLC) and form the corporation—all of these legal actions flow from filing the articles of conversion. Further, once the articles of conversion are filed, the assets and liabilities of the prior business are automatically transferred over to the new corporation under the laws of most states. In other words, you won't have to formally prepare a bill of sale or other legal paperwork to formally transfer the assets of the unincorporated business over to the corporation.

If you are planning to convert a partnership to a corporation, take a quick look at the forms download page on your state's corporate filing office website to see whether articles of conversion are available for use. If not, you may wish to browse your state's corporation law to see whether it contains a conversion statute that allows you to prepare and file articles of conversion. Again, always check with your tax adviser before deciding how to convert to a corporation, because different types of conversions can have different tax consequences. **Note:** Using a conversion form can have hidden tax consequences—see "Additional Considerations When Filing a State Entity Conversion Form," in Chapter 8.

CAUTION

Protect your limited liability after you incorporate. Incorporators need to exercise an extra measure of caution after converting an unincorporated business to a corporation to make sure the corporate limited liability shield works to protect them from personal liability for new corporate debts. The incorporators can be held personally liable to creditors who continue to extend credit to the business, if the creditors reasonably believe they are still dealing with an unincorporated business. To make sure this doesn't happen, once the unincorporated business is converted, the incorporators should send a friendly letter to each creditor of the prior business to let them know that the business has been converted to a corporation, which has assumed the debts of the prior business. A copy of each letter should be placed in the corporate records.

CAUTION

Sign in the name of the corporation. Once the business is converted to a corporation, corporate directors, officers, and employees should always sign business papers, notes, commitments, and correspondence in the name of the corporation in their capacity as corporate principals, not in their own names as they were accustomed to doing in their unincorporated business. For example, if Edith Frax and Jacque Rack, owners of Rackafrax Enterprises, convert their partnership to Rackafrax Enterprises, Inc., with Edith as CEO and Jacque as CFO, they should sign all corporate documents and correspondence in their corporate capacities only in the name of Rackafrax Enterprises, Inc., by Edith Frax, CEO or by Jacque Rack, CFO. For example:

Rackafrax Enterprises, Inc.,

By: _____

Edith Frax, CEO

Income Tax Consequences of Conversion

Converting a partnership to a corporation is a tax-free transaction, as long as the conversion meets the requirements of Section 351 of the Internal Revenue Code and its associated regulations. Chapters 6 and 7 discuss the main issues that arise when trying to achieve a tax-free incorporation of a prior unincorporated business.

Tax Filing Procedures

After converting a partnership to a corporation, the business is subject to corporate income taxes and must file an annual federal corporate income tax return, IRS Form 1120, *U.S. Corporation Income Tax Return*. Once incorporated, the owners who work in the business become corporate employees whose salaries can be deducted from corporate income.

Corporate income paid out as salaries is taxable to the owner-employees at their individual income tax rates. These payments are subject to payroll taxes, which the corporation withholds, reports, and pays. Income retained in the corporation is taxed at corporate income tax rates, and profits directly paid out to shareholder investors are taxed at a current dividend tax rate (15% under the current rules). For more information on corporate income and payroll tax filing procedures, see Chapter 4.

S Corporation Tax Election Procedures

When a corporation is formed, the IRS automatically treats it as a regular C corporation, which is subject to all of the corporate income tax rules contained in Subchapter C of Title 26 of the Internal Revenue Code. However, if the corporation and its shareholders qualify, the corporation can elect S corporation tax treatment by filing IRS Form 2553, *Election by a Small Business Corporation*. After this election is made, the profits, losses, deductions, credits, and other tax items of the corporation pass through the corporation and are allocated to the shareholders on their individual income tax returns. By making this filing, the owners will be taxed in a manner similar to the treatment they received as partners. (For more information on pass-through tax treatment, see Chapter 4.)

An S corporation owner who works in the business is treated pretty much the same as a partner in a partnership and normally does not qualify for tax and favored employee fringe benefits.

Self-Employment Tax

After incorporating, a general partner usually receives corporate profits in the form of a corporate salary, which is subject to Social Security and Medicare (FICA) taxes. After a partnership is incorporated, the corporation pays one-half of the FICA tax owed on the owner's (shareholder-employee's) wages, and the owner (shareholder-employee) pays the other half through payroll deductions from his or her corporate salary.

Self-employment tax rules for former limited partnerships usually do not change after incorporation. Any profits paid out by the corporation will be in the form of dividend payouts to the passive investors (the prior limited partners); these are not subject to FICA tax. But the investors will have to pay income tax on these payouts. (Their tax bills should be smaller after incorporation, because the dividends tax rate is lower than individual income tax rates for most investors.) However, the corporate tax rate also applies to corporate income paid out as dividends. In other words, dividends are not deductible by the corporation.

S Corporation Social Security Tax Break

If, after the conversion of a partnership to a corporation, the corporation elects S corporation tax treatment by filing IRS Form 2553, *Election by a Small Business Corporation*, profits of the corporation are automatically allocated to the shareholders. These automatically allocated profits are not subject to FICA tax.

Securities Laws Procedures

When you convert to a corporation, your new corporation will be issuing shares of stock (securities) to the former partners. This sale of securities must be registered under federal or state securities laws or must qualify from an exemption from these laws.

When shares are sold privately, without advertising, to people who will be active in running corporation (such as directors and officers) or to a small number of sophisticated investors who have sufficient experience in financial matters to protect their own interests, these sales usually qualify for securities law exemptions under state and federal law. See the appendix for contact information for your state's security law agency. ●

Converting an LLC to Another Entity

Once you form an LLC, you are not locked into it forever. After several years of successful business operations, you may wish to incorporate. Changing from an LLC to a corporation enables a business to attract capital or obtain the special tax breaks and incentives associated with corporate shares of stock.

It's also possible—though less common—that you may wish to head in a less formal direction and convert your LLC to a sole proprietorship or partnership. This chapter explains how an LLC can convert to a different legal entity, and the paperwork, tax, and securities law implications of such conversions.

Converting an LLC to a Corporation

Most LLC owners that convert their business to another type of entity choose to incorporate. There are at least four reasons why LLC owners might want to make this change:

- **Corporate income and tax splitting.** Accumulated business earnings and profits that are kept in the corporation are taxed at corporate tax rates of 15% and 25%, which are usually lower than the marginal (top) income tax rates of the LLC owners. If the owners keep income in the business, it may make sense to incorporate so that the retained business earnings are taxed at these lower rates.

- **Corporate stock.** Incorporating allows the owners to issue standard (common) and special (preferred) shares of stock, which makes the business more appealing to investors. Investment firms and public markets generally prefer to invest in corporations so that they can receive corporate stock in return for management, voting, and special dividend and liquidation rights. In addition, in family businesses, switching to the corporate form allows owners to create special classes of stock in anticipation of handing over the reins of control and ownership to the next generation.

- **Corporate equity-based employee plans.** The corporate structure allows owners to create incentives for key employees—such as tax-favored employee stock options, restricted stock bonus and purchase plans, and other equity-based employee incentives. These incentives are a unique, tax-favored benefit of the corporate form.

- **Built-in corporate structure.** Although the LLC has a formal structure, the corporate structure is often more suitable for larger businesses because it allows for separate management, supervisory, and investment roles. State corporation laws create separate director, officer, and shareholder positions, each with its own legal rights and responsibilities.

Legal Procedures

When converting from an LLC to corporation, you will need to take the following steps:

- **Review state law and termination provisions of your LLC operating agreement.** Most LLC operating agreements (and many state laws) require the unanimous consent of all members to dissolve the LLC. Even if your operating agreement or state law doesn't impose this requirement, it's a good idea to get each member's approval to terminate the LLC. After all, dissolution will affect each member's status as a business owner and may create tax consequences, so each member should carefully consider and approve the change.

- **File articles of dissolution.** Typically, you file legal papers called articles of dissolution (or something similar) with the state corporations section or division of the secretary of state's office in order to legally dissolve an LLC. Many states provide a fill-in-the-blanks articles of dissolution form online, which you can complete, print, and mail to the state filing office. (See the appendix.) Typically, you'll have to provide the name and address of the LLC, its date of dissolution, and a description of the membership vote obtained to approve the dissolution.

- **File articles of incorporation.** The owner(s) prepares and files articles of incorporation with the state corporate filing office. Standard articles forms are available online at most state corporate filing office websites. (See the appendix for information on finding your state's website.) Along with the articles, you send in the required filing fee, typically a flat fee or a charge based on the number and type of shares authorized in the articles.

- **Transfer assets and liabilities; issue shares.** Typically, the former LLC owners transfer the assets and liabilities of the LLC (or their ownership interest in the LLC) to the new corporation in return for shares of stock. The owners usually receive a percentage of shares in the corporation that is equal to their share of the assets (or ownership) of the prior partnership—for example, if four people owned equal shares of an LLC, each would receive one-fourth of the shares issued to owners. If any new co-owners (such as passive investors) are brought into the new corporation, they must pay cash or property for their shares of stock.

- **Revise licenses, permits, and registrations.** The owners should cancel any licenses and permits taken out in the name of the now-defunct LLC, then take out new permits and licenses in the name of the new corporation. If the corporation will do business under a name other than the one specified in its articles of incorporation, it should file a fictitious business name statement with the county clerk (or with the state corporations division in some states).

- **Get an EIN.** All corporations are required to obtain an employer identification number (EIN), whether or not they have employees.

> **TIP**
> **Find out if your state allows you to file articles of conversion.**
> In some states, a special one-step filing procedure is available to convert an LLC to a corporation using an articles of conversion form—a document that legally dissolves your LLC, forms your corporation, and typically transfers the

Additional Considerations When Filing a State Entity Conversion Form

Many state entity filing offices provide a simple entity conversion form to convert one type of entity to another. You check the appropriate boxes on the conversion form, add some boilerplate (as explained in the form instructions), file the form, and you're done. The new business is formed, the assets of the old business are transferred to the new business, and the old business is dissolved. All of this happens automatically by operation of law according to each state's entity conversion statute. What could be simpler?

Of course, nothing is quite so simple when law and taxes are involved, and both come into play when a business is converted to a new legal form.

Consider a common conversion—a co-owned LLC is converted to a corporation. Normally, an LLC-to-corporation conversion is tax-free if the prior business owners are in control of 80% or more of the stock of the new corporation (see IRS Publication 542, *Corporations*; and the book *Incorporate Your Business: A Legal Guide to Forming a Corporation in Your State* (Nolo)).

But there's more to it. IRS Revenue Ruling 84-111 puts partnership-to-corporation conversions into one of three categories (shown below). This Ruling applies to LLC-to-corporation conversions, since co-owned LLCs are treated like partnerships.

"Assets-Over" conversion. In this conversion, the LLC transfers its assets and liabilities "over" to the new corporation, the corporation issues its stock to the LLC, the LLC transfers the stock to its owners in proportion to their LLC capital interests, and then the LLC dissolves.

"Assets-Up" conversion. In an assets-up conversion, the LLC distributes its assets and transfers it liabilities "down" to its owners in proportion to their capital interests, the LLC dissolves, and then the owners transfer their individual share of received assets and liabilities "up" to the new corporation in return for a proportionate share of its stock.

"Interests-Over" conversion. In this conversion, the LLC owners transfer their LLC capital interests "over" to the new corporation in return for a proportionate amount of corporate stock, and then the LLC dissolves.

Additional Considerations When Filing a State Entity Conversion Form (cont'd)

Each of these conversion methods can have a different effect on the corporation's tax basis and holding period in the assets received. Further, LLC owners can end up with a different tax basis in their corporate stock, and each can end up with a different immediate tax result depending on the conversion method used. For instance, an owner may have to pay taxes at the time of the conversion.

OK, this is already sufficiently complicated, but there's more to consider. Revenue Ruling 2004-59 explains how the IRS treats an automatic conversion of an LLC to corporation through the filing of a state conversion form. This ruling says that when an entity treated as a partnership (again, which includes a co-owned LLC) is converted to a corporation through the filing of a state conversion form without an actual transfer of assets or interests, the IRS assumes the following steps occur, in the following order:

1. The partnership contributes all its assets and liabilities to the corporation in exchange for stock in such corporation.

2. The partnership liquidates, distributing the stock of the corporation to its partners.

This assumed sequence of events matches the sequence of events described in the assets-over conversion listed above, which means it's likely that the IRS will consider the conversion of an LLC to a corporation through a state conversion form filing to be an assets-over conversion. This leads to further complications that can have significant tax effects.

For example, Internal Revenue Code (IRC) Section 1244 allows business owners to treat worthless stock as an ordinary loss, which can be deducted against ordinary income on their tax returns. However, one of the requirements of using Section 1244 is that the shareholder claiming the loss must be the original owner of the stock. But if you re-read the description of an assets-over conversion, you'll see that the LLC entity, not its owners, is considered to be the original owner of the shares under that conversion scenario, and the corporation's shareholders are considered to be the second set of shareholders (they receive their shares from the dissolving LLC).

Additional Considerations When Filing a State Entity Conversion Form (cont'd)

The upshot is that the use of a simple state conversion form to convert an LLC to a corporation may eliminate the future ability of the corporation's shareholders to take a large deduction on their individual tax returns. Instead, the shareholders may be limited to claiming only a capital loss if their corporation fails. Since a capital loss can only be used to offset capital gains, the owners may be unable to deduct the loss on their capital investment, or may have to wait several years to do so.

Complications and unexpected tax results of this sort are why it's best to check with a tax adviser before making even the simplest type of filing with the state to form a business entity or convert an entity from one form to another.

LLC's assets to the new corporation. If such a form is available in your state, using it will minimize your paperwork requirements and save you time. Go to your state's website for additional information on available forms (see the appendix).

Income Tax Consequences of Conversion

Converting an LLC to a corporation is a tax-free transaction, as long as the conversion meets the requirements of Section 351 of the Internal Revenue Code. In fact, because the IRS treats a one-person LLC as a sole proprietorship, converting the LLC to a corporation is, for tax purposes, just the same as converting a sole proprietorship to a corporation.

Similarly, because a co-owned LLC is treated like a partnership under the Internal Revenue Code, converting a co-owned LLC to a corporation is the same, for tax purposes, as converting a partnership to a corporation.

A knowledgeable tax adviser should be able to help you qualify your conversion as a tax-free exchange under IRC Section 351. For more information on some of the issues that might come up in trying to achieve a tax-free incorporation of a prior unincorporated business, see Chapter 6.

Tax Filing Procedures

A co-owned LLC must file a final partnership tax return when it dissolves. A sole-owned LLC files its last Schedule C as part of the sole owner's 1040 individual income tax when the sole proprietorship is terminated. After the conversion to a corporation, the prior LLC owner or owners will report their corporate salaries as employee wages on their individual 1040 tax returns; these amounts will be taxed at the individual's regular graduated income tax rates. Investors who receive dividends from the corporation must also report this income on their individual income tax return, but dividend income currently is subject to a preferential 15% income tax rate in most cases.

After an LLC converts to a corporation, the business must file a corporate income tax return, IRS Form 1120, *U.S. Corporation Income Tax Return*. It also must obtain its own federal EIN.

Social Security Tax

Once a business is incorporated, each owner who works in the business will become a corporate employee. The corporation must withhold, report, and pay income and payroll taxes, including Social Security and Medicare (FICA) taxes. The total FICA tax rate for each employee is the same as the self-employment tax rate that applies to active owners in an LLC—currently, 15.3% of covered wages or self-employment income. However, after you incorporate, your corporation pays half of the FICA tax bill and you (the employee) pay the other half through payroll deductions from your corporate salary. Because you own the corporation, you will still be footing the entire tax bill, anyway—half out of your personal pocket, and half from your corporate pocket.

What Is a Dividend?

Many people assume that any money a corporation pays to its shareholders—except payments in exchange for services, such as corporate salaries—qualifies as a dividend. Although this is a sensible and common assumption, the rules are actually more complex. Under the Internal Revenue Code, only money paid out of the corporation's "earning and profits" (E & P) is treated as a dividend.

For tax purposes, E & P means the real money earned by a corporation. E & P is usually calculated by starting with the corporation's net taxable income, then making additions and subtractions to arrive at an accurate, real-world estimate of what the corporation has earned. For example, a corporation cannot deduct federal taxes paid from its taxable income, but these taxes are subtracted when calculating the corporation's E & P.

To be treated as a dividend, money must be paid out of the corporation's E & P. An additional wrinkle: Even if your corporation has an accumulated negative E & P balance carried over from prior years, if the corporation has positive E & P in the current year, profits paid out for the current year are treated as dividends (to the extent of this year's E & P). This means you can't use past E & P to offset current year E & P, and if you make a payout to shareholders in any year with positive E & P it will be subject to dividend tax treatment. This is called the "nimble dividend" rule. Even though the management might have thought that the payout will be treated as a return of capital (see below), it will be taxed to the shareholders as a "nimble dividend."

> **EXAMPLE:** Phil and Buster own Crud Busters, Inc., a corporate commercial office cleaning franchise. They are funded by a small investment group. Although the corporation lost money in its early years, the current year shows E & P of $70,000. The board decides to declare and issue a $50,000 total dividend to the shareholders. The payout will be treated as and taxed to the shareholders as a dividend (at the current 15% preferential dividends tax rate applied to most taxpayers), because the current E & P exceed the total dividend payout.

If a corporation makes a payout but does not have positive E & P for the current or past years, and the payout is made to shareholders in proportion to their

What Is a Dividend? (cont'd)

stockholdings, it will be treated as a return of capital. In this case, payout first reduces each shareholder's "basis" in his or her shares of stock. Then, and only then, if the payout is big enough to reduce a shareholder's basis to zero, the amount by which the payouts exceed the shareholder's basis will be taxed to the shareholder at capital gains tax rates.

EXAMPLE: In the early years, before Crud Busters has positive E & P, the investors are clamoring for a payout. The board agrees to make a distribution out of cash reserves. Fiona, an investor, gets $10,000 as her share of the distribution. Because the corporation has negative E & P for the current and past tax years, it isn't taxed to her as a dividend. Instead, the payout reduces her basis in her shares. Fiona's current basis in her shares is $15,000: the amount she originally paid for them. The $10,000 payout simply reduces her basis to $5,000, and she pays no tax on the distribution. If Crud Busters distributes another $10,000 to Fiona the following year (when it continues to have a negative E & P), the situation is different. This time, the first $5,000 of the payout reduces Fiona's current $5,000 basis in her shares to zero. The remaining $5,000 of the payout is taxed to Fiona at capital gains tax rates. If Fiona held her shares for more than one year, she must pay tax at the 15% long-term capital gains tax rate.

You may have noticed that the current dividend tax rate and the long-term capital gains tax rate are exactly the same: 15%. So why does it matter how the IRS characterizes a particular payout of corporate profits? There are two reasons:

- When a payout is treated as a return of capital, only the portion of the payout that exceeds the shareholder's basis in his or her shares is taxed; the entire amount of a dividend is always taxed.
- The current 15% dividend tax rate is scheduled to sunset (automatically repeal) after 2010. Unless Congress acts to extend it, dividends paid after 2010 will be taxed at each shareholder's marginal income tax rate, which is usually higher than the capital gains tax rate.

Securities Laws Procedures

If the former owners of the LLC transfer their interests in the prior LLC to the corporation in exchange for stock, this constitutes a "sale" of shares, which is subject to state and federal securities laws. Many small corporations can qualify these types of sales for an exemption from the securities laws—that is, they won't have to provide the disclosures and follow all the rules imposed by the securities laws to protect the interests of stock purchasers.

In some states, exemptions are applicable only if the prior owners get a proportionate stake in the new corporation equal to their share in the prior business. In all cases, make sure your "sale" of shares qualifies for both federal and state securities laws exemptions and that you file any exemption forms required. For resources for finding securities law information in your state, see the appendix.

Converting an LLC to a Sole Proprietorship

It's unusual for an LLC to convert to a sole proprietorship. If the LLC owner no longer wants legal liability protection or dislikes the red tape or cost of operating the LLC, however, he or she may decide to dissolve it. In addition, in rare cases, such as California's statutory LLC fee scheme, additional entity-level taxes may make the LLC an unappealing choice. (See "Check Out State LLC Annual Fees Before Forming an LLC," in Chapter 3.) Sometimes, a co-owned LLC is left with only one owner. In these cases, it is also unusual for the owner to convert to a sole proprietorship. The remaining member usually chooses to keep the LLC intact.

> ⊘ **CAUTION**
>
> **Wyoming LLC owners beware.** In almost every state, a co-owned LLC that dwindles down to one owner can continue operating as an LLC. In Wyoming, however, a two-member LLC will dissolve automatically when it is left with just one member, unless the LLC has elected to become a "flexible limited liability company" in its articles. For more information on each state's LLC formation and operation requirements, go to the state's business filing office website. (See the appendix.)

EXAMPLE: Carlos and Sasha own and operate their own personal training company, Toned Bones, LLC. The owners have good business smarts, and they market their services to local businesses. Before long, they carve out a niche providing custom training to corporate employees specifically geared to enhancing performance in different sports activities. Their business is successful, and they find themselves overwhelmed with calls from employees of corporate clients. They hire employees and sign up a crew of certified personal trainers as independent contractors to help them handle the workload.

After a year or so, Carlos is tired of working long hours and decides to retire in order to chase his ultimate dream: pursuing an acting career. Sasha is happy for Carlos, and over the course of a few phone calls, they reach an agreement for Sasha to buy out Carlos's LLC interest. As part of the agreement, Sasha will be allowed to continue the business as her sole-owned LLC, and she'll get to keep the Toned Bones name. Sasha decides to stay in business as an LLC. Even though she no longer needs to protect herself from liability for Carlos's business decisions and acts, she wants the LLC to protect her in the event of any client lawsuits (pulled muscles, claims of trainer negligence, and the like) as well as disputes with suppliers, gyms, and other companies that do business with her LLC.

Legal Procedures

An LLC owner that wants to convert to a sole proprietorship must take these steps:

- **Review termination provisions of LLC operating agreement.** All members should consent to the legal dissolution of the LLC. Most LLC operating agreements (and many state laws) require a unanimous vote of all members to approve a dissolution of the LLC. Even if your state's law and operating agreement don't require unanimous approval, you should get each member's approval to terminate the LLC. After all, a dissolution will affect each member's legal status as a business owner and can have tax consequences for each member, so it's important for everyone to agree to the change.

- **File articles of dissolution.** You must file paperwork with the state— typically with the corporations section or division of the secretary of state's office—to legally dissolve an LLC. Many states provide articles of dissolution or a similar LLC dissolution document (called a certificate of dissolution, articles of termination, or something similar) online for you to fill in, print, and mail to the state filing office. (See the appendix for information on finding your state's filing office website.) Typically, you will have to provide the name and address of the LLC, its date of dissolution, and a description of the membership vote obtained to approve the dissolution.

- **Revise licenses, permits, and registrations.** The sole proprietor (the remaining owner of the dissolved LLC) should cancel any licenses, permits, and registrations issued in the name of the LLC, then take out new permits and licenses in the name of the new sole proprietorship. If the sole proprietorship will do business under a name other than that of the owner, he or she must file a new fictitious business name registration. Some states also require the business to file a notice of dissolution in a newspaper—a newspaper that handles legal notices can tell you how to accomplish this routine filing.

> ! **CAUTION**
> **Some states impose additional LLC dissolution filing requirements.** Some states have special LLC dissolution filing requirements. For example, California requires all LLCs to file a certificate of cancellation to cancel the LLC's previously filed articles of organization. If the certificate does not indicate that the dissolution of the LLC was approved by all members, the LLC must also file a separate certificate of dissolution.

Income Tax Consequences of Conversion

The income tax consequences of converting an LLC to a sole proprietorship depend on whether the LLC is owned by one or more than one member.

One-Member LLCs

If the owner of a one-member LLC dissolves the LLC and continues the business as a sole proprietor, there are no federal income tax consequences associated with the change, because the IRS already treats a one-owner LLC as a sole proprietorship. As far as the IRS is concerned, there has been no change in the tax status of the business—both before and after the dissolution of the LLC, the profits and losses of the business are reported on the owner's 1040 Schedule C as the owner's profits and losses from the operation of a sole proprietorship.

Most states also treat a sole-owner LLC as a sole proprietorship for state income tax purposes. This means that many state tax agencies, like the IRS, will not treat the legal dissolution of a one-owner LLC as a change in the tax status of the business for state income tax purposes.

There's an exception to this general rule, however. In states that asses a separate entity-level tax on LLCs, the legal dissolution of the LLC will result in a change of tax treatment. After the dissolution, the business will not have to pay future LLC entity-level taxes or fees. States that asses an entity-level LLC tax or fee also typically require the LLC to file a final state LLC tax return and obtain a final LLC state tax clearance, which indicates that the LLC has paid all outstanding LLC fees and taxes, when it files its legal dissolution papers with the state. States that impose this requirement may enforce their final tax filing procedures by requiring the state corporate filing office to wait until the state tax office has issued a final state LLC tax clearance before filing the LLC's articles of dissolution.

Co-Owned LLCs

Under the federal tax law (and state tax law in most states), a co-owned LLC is taxed as a partnership. If the LLC legally changes to a sole proprietorship, the tax law treats the change as a tax termination of the partnership. This means that the owners must file a final partnership tax return for the LLC and may have to pay taxes. Thereafter, the continuing sole proprietor must report profits of the business on Schedule C, *Profit or Loss From Business*, on his or her 1040 individual income tax return.

Converting to a Smaller LLC

When a co-owned LLC loses one or more members, it may decide to change its business form—but it may also decide to continue doing business as an LLC. The tax consequences of this change depend on whether the LLC continues with a single owner or with more than one member.

Under the federal tax law (and state tax law in most states), a sole-owner LLC is taxed as a sole proprietorship, while a co-owned LLC is taxed as a partnership. When you change from a multiowner to a sole-owner LLC, the IRS will treat this change as if you had converted from a partnership to a sole proprietorship. The LLC will have to file a final partnership tax return, the prior co-owners of the LLC may have to pay income tax, and the remaining sole owner will begin filing a Schedule C with his or her IRS Form 1040 to report future LLC profits.

If your co-owned LLC loses one or more members but continues to operate as a co-owned LLC, you might think that there are no immediate tax consequences. After all, you are not legally converting your LLC to a sole proprietorship, and your LLC is still treated as a partnership by the IRS. However, federal (and state) tax law may require you and your co-owner(s) to pay tax when one or more members leave your co-owned LLC. Under Section 708 of the Internal Revenue Code, if more than 50% of a partnership's capital and profits interests changes hands during a 12-month period, the partnership is terminated for tax purposes. This means that the business must file a final partnership return, and each of the current and former partners may owe income tax. Because a co-owned LLC is taxed as a partnership, this tax termination rule applies to LLCs as well.

EXAMPLE: Venture Syndicates, LLC is a co-owned investment firm with five members, each of whom owns 20% of the business. If three of the members leave in a 12-month period, selling their interests back to the LLC or to other members, Section 708 comes into play (because 60% of the interests has changed hands during the 12-month period). The LLC has to file a final partnership tax return, the original five members may have to pay income tax, and the remaining two members have to file a partnership tax return for the reconstituted LLC.

Tax Filing Procedures

If an LLC converts to a sole proprietorship, the remaining sole owner of the business must report profits of the business on Schedule C, *Profit or Loss From Business*, on his or her individual income tax return. Of course, if the prior LLC had only one owner, the owner is already reporting LLC profits on a Schedule C (because a one-owner LLC is treated as a sole proprietorship for tax purposes), so the owner will not need to file any new tax forms. The owner continues to file a Schedule C to report and pay taxes on business profits.

Self-Employment Tax Status of Owner

A sole proprietor who is active in the business (as is usually the case) must pay self-employment tax on net profits of the business.

Securities Laws Procedures

Converting an LLC to a sole proprietorship should not present any immediate security law issues. In the typical case, there will not be a sale or change of ownership rights, so the securities laws should not come into play.

Of course, if the LLC owner brings in another person when the LLC is terminated—for example, if the sole owner of an LLC converts the LLC to a new partnership by dissolving the LLC and bringing another owner into the business—the securities laws may apply to this sale of a business interest to the new partner. If the new partner is a nonmanaging owner—for example, if the LLC is converted for some reason to a limited partnership that sells limited partnership interests to new owners —the securities law definitely will apply, since limited partnership interests are treated as "securities." See Chapter 6 for more information.

Converting an LLC to a Partnership

Although it isn't common, sometimes an LLC converts to a partnership. This conversion happens if the LLC is legally dissolved and the business is continued by two or more owners. This LLC-to-partnership conversion is fairly unusual—after all, why would LLC owners want to give up the legal liability protection of the LLC and operate as an unprotected partnership? Even if new owners are brought into the business, most would rather join the LLC than go into business with the new owners as a partnership.

Legal Procedures

If you decide to convert your LLC to a partnership, you must follow these steps:

- **Review termination provisions of LLC operating agreement.** All members should consent to the legal dissolution of an LLC. Most LLC operating agreements (and many state laws) require a unanimous vote of all members to approve a dissolution of the LLC. Even if your state's law and your LLC's operating agreement don't require unanimous approval, you should get each member's approval to terminate the LLC. A dissolution will affect each member's legal status as a business owner and can have tax consequences for each member, so you'll want to have everyone consider and approve the change.

- **File articles of dissolution.** You must file paperwork with the state—typically with the corporations section or division of the secretary of state's office—to legally dissolve an LLC. Many states provide articles of dissolution (sometimes called a certificate of dissolution, articles of termination, or something similar) online for you to fill in, print, and mail to the state filing office. (See the appendix for assistance in locating your state's filing office's website.) Most state forms ask you to provide the name and address of the LLC, its date of dissolution, and a description of the membership vote obtained to approve the dissolution.

- **Revise licenses, permits, and registrations.** The owners should cancel any licenses, permits, and registrations issued in the name of the LLC and take out new permits and licenses in the name of the new partnership. If the partnership will operate under a name other than that of the owners, it should file a new fictitious business name registration. Some states require the business to file a notice of dissolution of partnership in a newspaper—a newspaper that handles legal notices can tell you how to accomplish this routine filing.

- **Get an EIN.** You should get a new federal EIN on behalf of the partnership, even if it does not have employees. (Partners are not considered employees for payroll tax purposes.) This EIN must be used on partnership tax returns.

> **TIP**
>
> **Creating a limited partnership.** When an LLC dissolves and continues to do business as a general partnership, the owners don't have to file any formation paperwork with the state (although they will have to file articles of dissolution to formally end the LLC). However, if the owners wish to set up a limited partnership, they must file a certificate of limited partnership (or a similarly named document) with the state filing office. Many states provide ready-to-use downloadable forms for dissolving LLCs and forming limited partnerships; some may even provide a one-step conversion form. Check your secretary of state's website. (See the appendix.)

Income Tax Consequences of Conversion

There should be no significant tax consequences of converting an LLC to a partnership (due to its rarity, there are apparently no IRS rulings or pronouncements on this sort of conversion). The conversion should be seen by the IRS as a change in form only, and not a taxable event, just like the conversion of a partnership to an LLC. However, if you use the conversion to change ownership, profits, or voting or other interests, the transaction may trigger a tax termination of the LLC. You should get tax advice prior to making any sort of conversion, even if the transaction is simple and does not involve changing ownership interests, adding new owners, or making any sort of adjustment to the way you own and operate your business.

Tax Filing Procedures

When a co-owned LLC dissolves, it must file a final federal partnership tax return (remember, the IRS treats co-owned LLCs as partnerships for tax purposes). In most states that impose an income tax, LLCs also are treated as partnerships under state income tax law, so the LLC will have to file a final state partnership return as well. Some states also require LLCs to file a special LLC tax return; in these states, the LLC must file a final version of this return. The new partnership then files an initial partnership tax return with the IRS (and the state) to report its profits going forward.

Self-Employment Tax Status of Owners

Converting a co-owned LLC to a partnership doesn't change the self-employment tax status of the business owners who continue to own and run the business. If the business owners were active managers of the previous LLC, they had to pay self-employment taxes on their share of the LLC's profits. After the conversion to a partnership, the owners will still have to pay self-employment taxes on their share of the business profits.

Securities Laws Procedures

Converting an LLC to a partnership should not present any security law issues, as long as the new partnership owners were active owners in the prior LLC. These continuing owners are not investing in a new enterprise, nor are they relying on the expertise or work of others to realize a profit in the new partnership—which means that the transaction should not be considered the "sale of a security" that is subject to securities law regulation. However, if the prior LLC owners bring new owners into the business when they convert the LLC to a partnership, the securities laws will apply if any of the new owners are investing in the partnership and will not assume an active management role in the business. By definition, selling business interests to any nonmanaging owners—for example, to limited partners in a new limited partnership—is a sale of "securities" and must comply with federal and state securities laws.

What If Your LLC Loses *All* of Its Owners?

If a one-member LLC loses its only member (through death, disability, withdrawal of the member, or otherwise), the LLC will automatically dissolve, because state laws require an LLC to have at least one member. The mechanics of the dissolution vary from state to state, but most states give an LLC some time to find a new member before a legal dissolution of the LLC occurs.

Converting, Dissolving, and Selling a Corporation

The corporate business entity, with its limited liability protection, formal structure, and advantageous tax rules, is the final destination in the evolution of many businesses. There are occasions, however, when the owners/shareholders of a corporation may want to change their tax status, go out of business, or sell their stock or assets to a buyer—perhaps another corporation that will take over and continue the business or acquire the company's assets and goodwill—that is, its products, formulas, trade secrets, and brands. This chapter discusses these common corporate transformations and explains their legal and tax ramifications. We analyze the tax implications of converting a C corporation to an S corporation, we review the process of liquidating and dissolving a corporation, and we cover selling a corporation to noncorporate or corporate buyers.

Converting a C Corporation to an S Corporation

As explained in Chapter 1, an S corporation is a corporation that qualifies for pass-through tax treatment under the Internal Revenue Code (and state corporate tax statutes). Once a corporation elects S corporation tax status, the business becomes a pass-through entity. The corporation's income, losses, deductions, and so on pass through to the corporation's shareholders in proportion to their ownership share in the corporation—for example, a 10% shareholder reports 10% of the net profits or losses on his or her individual income tax return. The corporation itself no longer has to pay corporate taxes on its profits.

When you elect S corporation status, you are changing only the way the corporation is taxed, not its legal form. After you convert to an S corporation, your legal structure will remain the same, and you will have to follow the same rules and observe the same formalities as you did when you were a C corporation.

TIP

Consider adopting a shareholders' agreement. Though it isn't legally required, many corporation owners enter into a legal contract called a shareholders' agreement when they elect S corporation status. In such an agreement, the shareholders and their spouses commit not to do anything that would jeopardize the corporation's S tax status (such as sell shares to a person or entity who would not be a qualified S corporation shareholder—see below for more on S corporation shareholder limitations).

There are a number of tax requirements that a corporation must meet to elect S corporation tax treatment. Two of the most important requirements are:

- **S corporations may have only one class of stock.** Unlike a C corporation, an S corporation cannot issue preferred classes of stock to investors (which give those investors special voting rights not enjoyed by other shareholders), nor can they set up profit-and-loss sharing ratios among the owners that are disproportionate to their stock ownership percentages. In an S corporation, profits and liquidation proceeds must be paid out proportionately to each owner in relation to his or her ownership interest (stockholdings) in the corporation.

- **S corporations have limitations on ownership.** An S corporation may have only up to 100 shareholders (a husband and wife and certain other family members count as one shareholder), and all of them must be citizens or permanent residents of the United States. Although this limit should not present a problem for a privately held S corporation, don't plan on taking an S corporation public—the shareholder head-count will easily exceed the 100-shareholder limit. Nonresident aliens (citizens of foreign countries) and business entities, such as other corporations, LLCs, and partnerships, cannot be S corporation shareholders. These restrictions can be an obstacle to operating an international business, in which owners and investors (and their families) are often citizens of foreign countries. And the limitations on other businesses owning stock in an S corporation will make it tough for you to find major investors. Special rules sometimes allow other S corporations, trusts, estates, and nonprofits to own S corporation shares, but these types of entities are not the typical investors most corporations hope to attract.

> **TIP**
>
> **You don't have to be incorporated to make an S corporation tax election.** Under IRS tax classification rules (see Chapter 4), partnerships and LLCs can elect to be treated for federal tax purposes as a C corporation, without having to actually convert their businesses to a corporate entity. They make this election by filing IRS Form 8832, *Entity Classification Election*. Once an unincorporated business elects corporate tax treatment, it can then elect S corporation tax treatment if it meets the requirement. (The IRS has said that simply filing an S Corporation tax election is enough—the IRS will assume that the unincorporated business also meant to file an 8832 form to first elect corporate tax treatment. Check with your tax adviser for more information on using this one-step procedure.) Of course, it rarely makes sense for a business that already enjoys pass-through tax status to elect S corporation status, unless the active owners are adopting S corporation tax status to lower their self-employment taxes (which are owed on business profits allocated to the owners each year). If this feature of S corporation tax status is critically important to you, discuss this with your tax adviser.

Financial and Tax Consequences of an S Corporation Tax Election

There are some important financial and tax consequences, good and bad, when you convert from a C corporation to an S corporation.

Advantages

Some of the advantages of converting to an S corporation are:

- **Profits pass through to owners.** S corporation tax status can be a convenient way for an existing C corporation to pass profits and losses through to the owners for a period of years. If the corporation converts to an LLC to achieve a similar result, both the corporation and the individual owners may have to pay tax, as explained below.

> EXAMPLE: Clifford and Milly, owners of Next Big Thing, a start-up software company, form a corporation because they believe it will be the best entity to attract financing. They get seed money from Vance, a financier, in return for a sizable bundle of common stock shares in the corporation and a seat on the board. Vance insists that Next Big Thing make an S corporation election during the early tax years of the corporation. Vance wants the losses during the early years to pass through the corporation so that he can report them on his individual income tax return and use them to offset other investment income. Once the corporation starts earning money, he wants the profits to pass through the corporation and be paid out to him and the other shareholders, rather than being "locked in" the corporation and taxed at corporate income tax rates. Vance expects to terminate the S corporation tax election (a) after the corporation starts turning a profit, or (b) if the corporation issues a second class of preferred stock to a venture capital fund, a transaction that automatically terminates the S corporation election.

CAUTION

Switching back and forth between C corporation and S corporation status can create tax complications. If a C corporation has accumulated earnings and profits (E & P) when it elects S corporation tax status, this E & P is passed on to the S corporation as C corporation income that has not yet been distributed and taxed to the shareholders. To make sure that the corporations' shareholders ultimately pay income tax on these earnings, the S corporation is required to maintain an accumulated adjustments account (AAA), which tracks the amount of income earned and passed through to S corporation shareholders *after* the conversion to S corporation status. If the S corporation makes payouts to shareholders that exceed the AAA balance, the excess payouts will be treated as dividend payouts of the prior C corporation and will be taxable to the shareholders at dividend tax rates. This rule was created to prevent C corporations from "bailing out" accumulated earnings and profits tax-free by electing S corporation status.

- **Only one level of tax must be paid when the S corporation is sold or liquidated.** When an S corporation is sold or liquidated, only the shareholders—not the corporation—must pay tax. (When a C corporation is sold, as explained below, both the C corporation and its shareholders may have to pay income taxes.) Shareholders will owe tax only if the sales proceeds they receive exceed their basis in corporate stock (usually, the price the shareholder paid for the stock). This tax break does not apply if the S corporation operated as a C corporation within ten years of its liquidation date, and its assets appreciated during the time it was a C corporation. This exception explains why it may be a good idea to convert a C corporation to an S corporation *before* corporate assets appreciate.

> **EXAMPLE:** Prime Properties, Inc., owned by Patricia and Pauline, elected S corporation status immediately after its incorporation. When it dissolves, the corporation sells its remaining real property for $150,000. The corporation's basis in this property is $70,000, so it calculates a gain of $80,000 on the sale. Half of this gain ($40,000) is allocated to each of the shareholders and taxed on their individual income tax returns at long-term capital gain tax rates. Let's assume that each owner has a basis of $35,000 in her shares. The passed-through $40,000 of S corporation gain increases the basis each

shareholder has in her shares to $75,000 ($35,000 + $40,000 = $75,000). Each shareholder received $75,000 in the liquidation of the corporation—half of the $150,000 proceeds from the sale of property. Patricia and Pauline do not owe any additional tax when they receive the proceeds. They would owe tax when the proceeds are distributed only on any amount that exceeds their income tax basis in their shares. Because their basis is equal to the total payout, this is a tax-free transaction.

- **S corporation status can lower self-employment taxes.** S corporation profits that are automatically allocated to the shareholders (as opposed to profits paid out as salary to the owners who work in the business) are not subject to self-employment tax. This can be an advantage for an S corporation owner (as compared to an active owner of an LLC, who must pay self-employment tax on all profits allocated to him or her).

> **EXAMPLE:** Charlie owns C-Thru Screw Corp., a company that fabri-cates transparent plastic screws for electronic component subsystems and assemblies. Now that federal individual income tax rates are lower and self-employment tax rates are higher than when Charlie started out, Charlie wants all corporate profits to pass through his corporation to him. Charlie normally gets a $100,000 salary from his corporation, and any remaining profits stay put in the corporation.
>
> Charlie's tax adviser, Denise, suggests making an S corporation tax election and lowering his corporate salary to $60,000. The remaining S corporation profits that are automatically allocated to Charlie will not be subject to self-employment tax (although his $60,000 salary will be). Denise tells Charlie that if he lowers his salary any more, he risks having his salary reduction challenged by the IRS as a Social Security tax evasion strategy. For example, if Charlie's return is audited and the IRS can show that Charlie's salary is significantly lower than

what corporate executives get for running businesses similar to Charlie's, the IRS can make Charlie pay self-employment tax on the amount of salary it claims he should have earned, plus interest and penalties. Denise also advises amending the corporation's bylaws to require the distribution of all net profits to the corporation's shareholders after the close of each corporate tax year. By doing this, Charlie gets all remaining corporate profits (after payment of his salary and other corporate expenses) free and clear of self-employment tax.

Note: Although Charlie was determined to elect S corporation tax status to lower his self-employment tax liability, most business owners will decide it is not worth the time, trouble, and risk of IRS challenge to elect S corporation tax status for this reason alone. For most business owners, paying Social Security/self-employment tax on salaries and profits earned in a business is simply an additional cost of doing business and, more significantly, a way to help make sure that their retirement is adequately funded.

Disadvantages

Two important disadvantages of choosing S corporation status are:

- **S corporations that previously operated as C corporations can, in some cases, lose S corporation status if they earn excess passive income.** Sources of "passive" income include rents, royalties, dividends, interest, and the like. Under technical rules, a business can lose its S corporation status if (1) it previously operated as a C corporation, during which time it accumulated earnings and profits that were inherited by the S corporation, and (2) the S corporation earns 25% or more of its income from passive income sources for three consecutive years.

- **S corporation owners can deduct fewer business losses than owners of other types of pass-through tax entities.** S corporate shareholders are more restricted in the extent to which they can use the corporation's debt to help reduce their tax bills. Entity-level debt includes money borrowed by the business or debts incurred by the corporation in connection with the purchase of property, such as a mortgage taken out on real property owned by the corporation. The tax rules about this issue are very technical, but you should be aware that you will be more restricted than owners of LLCs, sole proprietorships, or partnerships in your ability to use corporate debt to increase your tax basis in your shares.

> **TIP**
>
> **For most newly formed businesses, an LLC is a better choice than an S corporation.** As a general rule, if you want to form a small, privately held business with limited liability protection and pass-through tax treatment, you'll be better off as an LLC instead of forming a corporation and then making an S corporation tax election. Besides being easier to form and maintain, an LLC—unlike an S corporation—can be owned by individuals and entities and does not come with ownership restrictions. It also offers better opportunities for its owners to use business debt to increase their tax basis in shares. For a detailed explanation of the differences between S corporations and LLCs, see Chapter 1.

S Corporation Election Procedures

To make an S corporation tax election, you must file IRS Form 2553, *Election by a Small Business Corporation.* Once you elect S corporation status, the corporation must file an S corporation information tax return, IRS Form 1120-S, *U.S. Income Tax Return for an S Corporation.* The corporation must also prepare a Form 1120-S Schedule K-1, *Shareholder's Share of Income, Deductions, Credits, etc.,* for each shareholder, which shows the allocated profits, losses, or other tax items (deductions, credits, and the like) that are passed through to each shareholder at the end of the corporate tax year.

The S corporation election terminates automatically if and when the corporation fails to meet the S corporation eligibility requirements (for example, when it brings on shareholders that are other business entities or citizens of foreign countries). S corporation status will also terminate if a majority of the shareholders agree to revoke it. If a corporation makes an S corporation tax election and then terminates or revokes it, the corporation cannot reelect S corporation tax status for five years.

> **TIP**
> **States typically follow the IRS's lead.** If a corporation has made a valid federal S corporation tax election, states that impose corporate and individual income taxes typically accept this status for state corporate income tax purposes. In these states, corporate profits are not taxed to the S corporation at state corporate income tax rates but are passed through to the shareholders and taxed at state individual income tax rates.

Security Law Considerations

Electing S corporation tax status seldom involves the issuance of new shares of stock and, therefore, does not trigger any new obligations under federal and state securities laws.

Liquidating and Dissolving a Corporation

The owners of a small corporation may eventually decide that it's time to shut down their corporation and move on to other pursuits. To do this, the owners liquidate and dissolve the corporation, typically by selling its remaining assets, distributing the cash proceeds to creditors and shareholders, and then filing formal dissolution papers with the state. (The section "Selling a Corporation," below, discusses the issues that arise when a corporation is sold. These sales may or may not involve a dissolution of the corporation.)

Legal Procedures for Dissolution

In order to dissolve a corporation, the owners must prepare and file articles of dissolution (or a similarly titled document, such as a certificate of dissolution) with the state corporate filing office (typically, the corporations division of the secretary of state's office). As part of the state dissolution process, the corporation must pay any remaining state corporate income tax and pay or provide for payment to creditors of the corporation. The corporation can then distribute any remaining assets to shareholders in proportion to their stock interests (also taking into account any special liquidation preferences attached to preferred shares of stock).

A notice of the dissolution typically must be published in a legal newspaper, and shareholders as well as creditors can usually ask a court to oversee the dissolution process to make sure it happens smoothly and in conformance with state corporate law. For more on the legal formalities of corporate dissolution, see your state's corporate filing office website. (See the appendix.)

Income Tax Consequences of Dissolution

When a corporation dissolves, the corporation must file final state and federal corporate income tax returns and pay any remaining taxes due. Both the corporation and its shareholders may owe tax. For example, the corporation may owe income tax if its assets appreciated over its lifespan (if the corporation sells its assets for more than the corporation's income tax basis in the assets, for example), or if the corporation has to recapture depreciation previously taken on its liquidated assets. The shareholders also may have to pay income tax if the amount of cash or value of property they receive on liquidation exceeds their individual income tax basis in their shares. Special tax breaks are available when one corporation is sold to another as part of a tax-free reorganization.

TIP

The potential for double-level tax liability applies only to C corporations. S corporations usually do not pay a separate level of income tax when they dissolve. Typically, only their shareholders are liable for tax on liquidation or sale of the corporation.

Unincorporation Procedures

Owners of corporations occasionally desire to "unincorporate" their business and convert (or revert) to an LLC, partnership, or sole proprietorship. (This scenario is very rare.) Although some of the procedures for converting a corporation to another form of business entity are similar to the procedures for terminating a corporation, there are also some important differences:

- **Legal procedures.** States often provide a streamlined conversion or merger form that allows a corporation to simultaneously dissolve and convert to (or merge into) another type of entity, such as an LLC or limited partnership. (Because no state filing is required to form a sole proprietorship or general partnership, states do not provide forms to convert corporations into these entities.) If a conversion form is provided, it can streamline the process—in one filing, you can dissolve the corporation, form the unincorporated entity, and transfer over corporate assets and liabilities to the unincorporated entity.

- **Tax effects.** There are no special tax breaks or deferrals available for converting a C corporation to an unincorporated entity. For example, unlike other conversion scenarios—such as converting an LLC to a corporation—taxes on the conversion cannot qualify for deferral. At the time of the conversion, just as in a simple corporate dissolution scenario (discussed above), both the corporation and its shareholders may owe tax.

TIP

Distributions of cash and property on corporate liquidation are not treated as dividends. Even if a corporation has current or accumulated earnings and profits when it liquidates, the payout of these profits to shareholders is not treated as a dividend (or taxed at dividend tax rates—see Chapter 8). Instead, the liquidating payout is treated as a payment in exchange for a shareholder's stock. This means that the shareholder will owe tax only on any amount by which the payment exceeds his or her basis in the shares, not on the whole payout amount. This is a tremendous tax benefit. Also, the excess is taxed at capital gains tax rates—but because these rates are currently equal to the dividend tax rate, there's no special advantage here.

Social Security Tax

When a corporation dissolves, the owners must file final federal and state payroll tax returns and make all final Social Security and Medicare tax deposits for themselves and other corporate employees.

Securities Laws Procedures

The securities laws usually don't apply to the dissolution of a corporation in which the remaining assets of the corporation are distributed to shareholders in proportion to their shareholdings

However, state corporate law does provide legal mechanisms to ensure that shareholders and the corporation are treated fairly during the liquidation and dissolution of a corporation, such as court supervision of dissolution proceedings. In addition, disgruntled owners may bring shareholder derivative lawsuits against any person who mismanages the liquidation and dissolution of the corporation.

In corporate mergers and consolidations (in which corporate stock or assets are sold to another corporation in exchange for shares in the purchasing corporation), the securities laws do apply, of course. State corporation law typically provides certain procedural rights to those who dissent from the merger.

Selling a Corporation

Rather than shutting down their operations altogether, corporations are often acquired by other businesses—and these sales have important tax and legal implications. Below, we discuss situations when a noncorporate buyer acquires stock or assets of a corporation. We also discuss special legal and tax provisions that apply when a corporation is sold to another corporation as part of a tax-free corporate reorganization—a process that involves big tax breaks and incentives.

Selling a Corporation to a Noncorporate Buyer

When a corporation is sold, the process generally falls into one of two categories. In one scenario, the buyer wants the corporation's assets (for example, the seller's brand and other intangible assets) but does not want to continue operating the corporation. In this case, the corporation is usually dissolved. In the second scenario, the buyer purchases the corporation's stock in order to continue operating the corporation. In this case, the corporation stays alive and is not legally dissolved, although shareholders (and typically management) change.

There are legal and tax differences between a corporate sale of assets and stock. Here's a brief summary.

Asset Sales

In an asset sale, the corporation is legally dissolved, and for C corporations, both shareholders and the corporation itself may owe taxes. The corporate-level tax applies not just to the sale of tangible (physical) assets but also to its intangible assets, such as "goodwill." Goodwill is an intangible asset that represents the attractiveness of the business and its assets to the buyer (reputation, brand, future sales, and growth potential)—it's usually measured as the amount by which the corporation's sale price exceeds the fair market value of its assets. This "value-added" or extra amount is also subject to corporate-level and shareholder-level taxes when a corporation is sold.

In an asset sale, the buyer gets a "stepped-up" basis in the purchased assets equal to the amount of the purchase price allocated to each asset. This permits the buyer to take greater amounts of depreciation on depreciable assets after the sale, which can lower taxes.

The purchase price in an asset sale must be allocated between physical assets and goodwill. This allocation has tax effects for both the buyer and the seller—for example, the allocation can affect how much depreciation (or amortization) the buyer takes later on purchased assets. Talk to your tax adviser for information on these complicated rules.

Another reason why buyers may prefer an asset sale is that by buying only the assets (not the stock) of a selling corporation, the buyer avoids successor liability for claims against the selling corporation. (See "Successor Liability," below.)

Stock Sales

In a standard stock sale, the corporation is not dissolved. It is continued by the new owners, who typically take over management. The new owners vote in a new board to take over management, and this board, in turn, appoints new officers.

In this buy-out scenario, generally only the shareholders, not the corporation itself, have to pay tax on the stock transaction. Each shareholder pays capital gains tax on the amount by which the sale price exceeds the shareholder's basis in his or her shares. The owners of private corporations generally prefer to sell their stock rather than the assets of their corporation, because a stock sale results in only one level of tax to the shareholders; the proceeds from the sale are not reduced by any corporate-level tax liability.

Successor Liability

Buyers in stock sales have to worry about "successor liability," a legal doctrine that can make the buyer in a corporate stock sale liable for claims made against the selling corporation *after* the sale. In other words, the buyer can be liable for improper activities that occurred prior to the purchase of the business, if legal claims based on those activities are brought after the purchase.

The owners of the selling corporation can "indemnify" the buyer against these future claims. Under indemnification, the selling shareholders promise to pay any claims made against the buyers for acts or liabilities that occurred prior to the sale and often are asked by the buyers to deposit money in an escrow account to pay these potential claims. Sometimes, even the remote possibility of having to face successor liability may lead a buyer to insist on purchasing just the assets, not the stock, of a selling corporation.

RESOURCE
Want to know more about drafting a sales agreement? For information on creating a basic agreement for the sale of a business, which includes structuring a basic corporate sale-of-assets or sale-of-stock agreement, see *The Complete Guide to Selling a Business*, by Fred Steingold (Nolo).

Selling a Corporation to Another Corporation

Often, a C corporation sells a controlling interest in its shares or substantially all of its assets to another C corporation, usually in return for stock in the buying corporation (plus cash, in many cases, to the shareholders of the selling corporation). This transaction is known as a reorganization, as distinguished from a conversion, when an owner abandons one form of business for another—for example, when business owners convert their LLC or partnership into a new corporation.

Reorganizations that comply with IRS rules, also adopted in the tax code of many states, can qualify as tax-free transactions to the selling and buying corporation as well as to their shareholders. There are a number of ways to qualify for this tax-free status, but you'll need expert legal and tax help to do it right. A properly executed reorganization corporate exit strategy is one of the potential benefits of forming a corporation. The owners create value for corporate shareholders and then allow the shareholders to sell their appreciated interests to another corporation at the least possible tax cost.

TIP

Reorganization tax rules benefit only corporations. The tax-free reorganization rules in the Internal Revenue Code apply only to corporations, not to unincorporated businesses (unless they have elected corporate tax treatment).

Types of Reorganizations

There are two classes of reorganizations: merger and nonmerger.

- **Merger reorganizations.** In a merger reorganization, a buying corporation purchases the stock of a selling corporation. The selling corporation dissolves, and its assets and liabilities are transferred to the buying corporation. One advantage of a merger is that the transfer of the assets and liabilities occurs automatically, without the need for piles of legal paperwork (offers, bills of sale, and other transfer documents). The selling corporation liquidates and dissolves automatically when it merges into another corporation. The seller doesn't have to file separate liquidation and dissolution forms with the state. There are several special types of mergers recognized under state corporate law—for example, short-form mergers that are streamlined to facilitate the merger of a wholly owned or mostly owned subsidiary corporation into a parent corporation, often called a rollup. There also are special forms and procedures for triangular mergers, the merger of a corporation into a subsidiary of its parent corporation.

> **TIP**
> **Interspecies merger procedures.** States also have special procedures and forms to merge a corporation into an existing unincorporated entity, such as an LLC or limited partnership. These corporate-to-noncorporate mergers are called "interspecies" mergers and often involve significant tax costs. (See the section "Liquidating and Dissolving a Corporation," above, for more information on taxes that may be owed when converting a corporation to an unincorporated entity.)

- **Nonmerger reorganizations.** There are various types of nonmerger reorganizations. For example, an exchange reorganization occurs when a selling corporation sells a controlling interest (the majority of its shares) to another corporation in return for *its* shares. A sale of assets reorganization occurs when substantially all of the assets of a selling corporation are sold to another corporation in exchange for the buyer's shares. As opposed to merger reorganizations, exchange or sale-of-asset reorganizations do not include the liquidation of the selling corporation and its legal merger into the buying corporation.

Reorganization Procedures

Typically, the board of directors of both the selling and buying corporation must approve a plan of merger or reorganization, and the shareholders of the selling and often the buying corporation also must approve. Typically, at least a majority of all outstanding shareholders entitled to vote—and sometimes more, such as two-thirds of each class of outstanding shares entitled to vote—must approve the plan.

Dissenters from the plan—that is, shareholders who vote against the sale but who don't have sufficient votes to block it—usually get special dissenters' rights. For example, a state may provide that if 5% or more of the selling corporation's shareholders object, all dissenters can require the selling corporation to redeem (buy back) their shares at their current fair market value, rather than having to swap them for shares of the buying corporation per the terms of the reorganization. If the corporation resists the dissenting shareholders' demands for a buy-back, the dissenters can enforce their rights by bringing a lawsuit against the corporation in state court. If the shares are traded on a national securities exchange, dissenters typically do not get buy-back rights, because they can readily sell their shares at current market value on the public securities markets.

Each state provides its own forms and procedures for implementing corporate mergers and other reorganizations. These forms are usually available on the state corporate filing office's website (typically, the corporations division of the secretary of state's office). Reorganization forms, such as a certificate of merger, typically require the filer to state that the legal requirements for a corporate merger or other organization have been met. A copy of the merger or other reorganization agreement or plan certified by a corporate officer usually must be attached to the filing. And, of course, states that impose a corporate income or franchise tax typically require the disappearing corporation in a merger—the corporation that is merged into the acquiring corporation—to obtain a final clearance from the state tax agency certifying that all corporate income or franchise taxes have been paid, prior to the effective date of the proposed merger.

Income Tax Consequences of Corporate Reorganizations

In a tax-free reorganization, the selling and buying corporations do not pay tax on the transaction. Instead, the buying corporation takes over the assets and liabilities of the selling corporation and the tax attributes associated with these assets. For example, the selling corporation's basis in each transferred asset is carried over and becomes the buying corporation's basis in the assets. In effect, tax on the sale of the transferred assets is deferred (put off) until the buying corporation sells the assets in a taxable sale.

Typically, in a tax-free "Type A" reorganization (so-called because it is described in IRC Section 368(a)(1)(A)), the shareholders can receive cash as well as stock in the buying corporation in return for the sale of their shares in the selling corporation. If the shareholders receive stock only, they pay no tax on the transaction. Instead, they get a basis in their new shares equal to their basis in their old shares. When they sell their new shares, the shareholders pay capital gains tax on any amount by which the sale proceeds exceed their carried-over basis in the new shares.

If a shareholder in a Type A reorganization receives cash for his or her shares from the buying corporation, any cash amount that exceeds the shareholder's basis in the shares will be taxed at capital gains rates. The IRS has said that the buying corporation in a Type A reorganization can pay up to one-half of the purchase price in cash and one-half in its shares when it buys out the shareholders of the selling corporation without risking the tax-free nature of the deal. Many tax practitioners think it's possible to have an even greater proportion of cash to shares in the buyout mix—for example, from 55% to 60% in cash and only 45% to 40% in stock of the selling corporation—and still meet the technical requirements of a Type A tax-free reorganization. If you're looking into this type of arrangement, you will definitely need help from an experienced corporate tax professional.

There are additional types of tax-free reorganization (Types B through G) and numerous variations that a sale of corporate assets or stock can take to qualify for a tax-free reorganization and avoid taxes. Corporate tax advisers can create customized tax-favored corporate reorganization strategies to eliminate or minimize tax liabilities.

Securities Laws Procedures

When newly issued shares of the buying corporation are exchanged for shares of the selling corporation, both entities need to comply with federal and state securities laws. This means you will have to register the issuance or exchange of securities with the state and the federal Securities and Exchange Commission, unless a specific exemption for the exchange or issuance is provided under state and federal law. Even if an exemption is available, you still may have to file a notice of exemption form with the state and federal agencies.

The securities law issues and requirements are complex. You will need the help of an experienced corporate lawyer, who can prepare and file the legal paperwork for the reorganization and help you with the securities law filings, notices, or exemption forms. ●

Business Choice and Conversion Scenarios

revious chapters provided you with basic legal and tax rules for choosing between an LLC or a corporation (or other business entity) and converting from one type of entity to another. This chapter pulls all of this information together, in a form that should give you some ideas about the best way to structure your ideas. Five fictional examples are presented to illustrate common business scenarios. Hopefully, one of these scenarios will shed some light on your own business entity decision:

- A start-up business chooses its business form.

- Two business owners seek a major investment from a relative.

- A business owner wants lower annual taxes and a structured business hierarchy.

- A company hopes to attract outside investors.

- A business moves from sole proprietorship to LLC to corporation.

Fast Food Fusion: A Start-Up Business Chooses a Business Form

Gil and Vera both work as chefs. They decide to quit their salaried jobs and strike out on their own by opening a multicuisine drive-through restaurant. They reject Gil's first choice for a business name, Quick Quisine, after Vera searches the Internet and learns that another food company is already using it. Rather than engage in a potential name battle with a national company, Vera suggests Fast Food Fusion, a safer choice, which Gil also likes. Their relatives express a willingness to invest in the new enterprise. Gil and Vera appreciate their generosity, but the two chefs are concerned that their relatives also may want a voice in management. The old adage, "Too many cooks can spoil the broth," gives them pause. They decide that they'd rather bring in their relatives as silent investors, who will write the checks and stay out of the kitchen.

What's the best business entity form for the owners and their investors? Here's a menu of the choices available to Gil and Vera, and a summary of how each fits—or doesn't fit—their situation and preferences:

- **Partnership.** A general partnership is not a good choice, because each investor—even the relatives whom Gil and Vera would like to keep out of the kitchen—automatically becomes a managing partner. Also, each of the owners, including the investors, is personally liable for business debts.

- **Limited partnership.** A limited partnership is a better choice than a regular partnership—the investors can be made limited partners who will not be personally liable for business debts or have an active voice in managing the business. However, the limited partnership still presents problems, the biggest of which is that Gil and Vera, as managing partners, will be personally liable for business debts.

- **Limited liability company.** The LLC, with its limited personal liability, appears to be the right match for Gil and Vera. They can set up a manager-managed LLC—Gil and Vera will have management responsibility, while the investors will become LLC nonmanaging members with a right to profits and a percentage of the sales proceeds when and if the LLC is sold. Finally, the LLC will provide them with pass-through tax treatment, which they both desire. (For more on LLC and corporate taxation, see Chapter 4.)

- **C corporation.** Gil and Vera could incorporate and serve as the directors and principal officers of the business, while the investors participate as shareholders. This legal structure would meet Gil and Vera's needs, but it is more complicated than Gil or Vera requires— they do not want to hold director and shareholder meetings each year, for example. Also, Gil and Vera want all income and expenses to pass through the business and be paid out to them as their share of the profits. That's not possible if they establish a C corporation.

- **S corporation.** Setting up an S corporation will prove more complicated than setting up a regular C corporation. To form an S corporation, the owners would have to set up a regular C corporation, then elect S corporation tax treatment with the IRS. The end result will be that the corporation achieves pass-through tax treatment, but the owners will still have to comply with corporate formalities (annual meetings) and make sure that their investors meet the S corporation shareholder requirements (they must all be U.S. citizens, for example).

The final verdict: For Gil and Vera, the LLC is the best choice. It will give them limited liability, pass-through tax treatment, and day-to-day control over the business.

Bill and Barbara Seek Investment From a Relative

Bill and Barbara, having sent the last of their children off to college, decide it's time to pursue their dream of opening a bed and breakfast on the northern California coastline. However, after taking a long, hard look at their financial situation, they agree that they will need to set aside more money than they had planned as a contingency fund to handle future expenses, such as tuition increases and emergency funds for their children's college expenses.

Bill calls his Aunt Bertha to discuss his plans and concerns. Aunt Bertha is a well-to-do and sophisticated investor and has been a supportive relative and good friend to Bill and Barbara over the years. Bill tells Bertha that he and Barbara are thinking of setting up a bed and breakfast, but they are worried that they might be stretching themselves too thin financially. They also need advice on the best business type to form to help them limit their legal, financial, and tax exposure.

Bertha advises the couple that they should form a corporation or an LLC, either of which would provide limited personal liability to the couple for business debts and claims. Bill and Barbara like the idea of limiting their liability, but which business choice, the LLC or corporation, is best for them? Bertha prefers the LLC and explains the benefits and drawbacks of each choice:

- **Limited liability company.** Bertha advises Bill and Barbara to go with an LLC, because it's easy to set up, and Bill and Barbara don't need all the legal and financial trappings of a corporation. She tells Bill she would be willing to invest start-up cash in return for an interest in the LLC. She does not want to be a voting member or manager, but she expects to receive profit distributions and wants the LLC operating agreement to specify that she will be paid profits first, before any allocated profits are paid out to the members. After she is paid her share of allocated profits, Bill and Barbara can receive at least enough to pay taxes on income allocated and taxed to them each year. Bertha explains that any initial start-up losses will flow though to the owners, and she can use her share to offset other investment income. Further, Bertha explains that the mortgage the LLC takes out for the B & B property will increase each LLC investor's "basis" in his or her LLC ownership interest, which means that each may be able to take more losses on his or her individual income tax return if the LLC loses money in the early years.

- **C corporation.** Bertha explains that she is not interested in investing if Bill and Barbara decide to form a corporation instead of an LLC. In a corporate entity, business income would be diminished by corporate income taxes. Corporate losses would not flow through to her as an investor. She knows that buying real estate in the name of a C corporation is generally not a good idea, because both the corporation and its shareholders will have to pay income tax if the property appreciates, the corporation or its assets are sold, and the proceeds are distributed to the shareholders. Bertha wants to help out Bill and Barbara no matter what they decide to do, however. If they decide to form a corporation, she won't invest in its stock but will lend them money under an interest-only demand note, payable in full by the corporation at the end of five years.

- **S corporation.** Bertha is not keen on the idea of investing in an S corporation even though it's a pass-through entity. She knows that her basis in an S corporation, unlike her basis in an LLC, will not increase if the business takes on debt, such as a mortgage on real property owned by the S corporation.

Bill and Barbara decide to follow Aunt Bertha's advice, after checking with their tax adviser, and they file articles of organization for Bill & Barb's B & B, LLC, then jump in the car and drive north to talk to real estate agents and scout out likely locations and properties (after calling the children to let them know they'll be out of town for a week or two).

Soaring Duck Designs Seeks Lower Taxes and a Structured Hierarchy

Mandrake is a talented mechanical engineer who built up his small, sole proprietorship manufacturing business, Soaring Duck Designs, to a 15-employee business in a reconditioned factory building. Profits are increasing as the business finds new retail outlets and distributor channels for its products. But managing the day-to-day business is taking a toll on Mandrake. He is unhappy serving as designer, owner, and day-to-day crisis-manager. Cash flow is Mandrake's constant nemesis— meeting the end-of-the-month payroll and 30-day accounts payable due dates keeps Mandrake awake through many nights.

Often, Mandrake must dig into his own pockets to replenish petty cash and meet other business emergencies. Constant demands for his personal attention leave him little time to do what he likes best: sitting down with paper and protractor and creating or improving his company's product designs. The unending requests for personal cash outlays in the business also ensure that he is left with little to take home as his so-called "100%" stake in the profits.

Mandrake complains to his tax adviser and good friend, Fenton, that his personal taxes are high but his real share of the profits is low because most profits are reinvested in the business. He also admits that he is getting tired of being chief cook and bottle washer in his business. He explains to Fenton that he is considering selling his business so that he can get back to doing what he loves, designing better products.

Fenton believes that Mandrake should convert his sole proprietorship to another business form, and he weighs the two most likely choices, LLC or corporation:

- **C corporation.** Fenton favors the C corporation as the entity of choice to solve Mandrake's immediate problems. He explains that incorporating can (a) protect Mandrake from personal liability for business debts and claims; (b) allow Mandrake to avoid paying high marginal individual income tax on profits left in the business; (c) help organize the business into separate management, officer, and investor roles; and (d) allow Mandrake to delegate business titles, responsibilities, and accountabilities to others, letting Mandrake share day-to-day supervisory chores with others in corporate management. Also, the corporate form will help ensure that Mandrake actually gets paid—he will become one of the employees of his corporation, entitled to a regular salary paid out in the form of a regular paycheck on scheduled paydays. Finally, Fenton mentions that adopting the corporate form can help Mandrake grow his business into a bigger enterprise if Mandrake wants to add investors later.

- **Limited liability company.** Like the corporation, the LLC will protect Mandrake from personal liability, but forming an LLC will not change Mandrake's financial situation. He will still have to pay marginal individual income taxes on profits left in the business. In addition, the informal business structure of the LLC does not provide the "corporate camouflage" Mandrake needs to let him blend in better as one of several members of an integrated management team.

- **S corporation.** Like the LLC, the S corporation offers Mandrake no relief from his financial problems. Because the business is still a pass-through tax entity, Mandrake will continue having to pay marginal individual income taxes on profits left in the business.

Mandrake follows Fenton's advice and incorporates. The tax and legal advantages meet Mandrake's requirements, but the big personal plus is that Mandrake, as the CEO and an employee of his company, now shares the managerial workload with other officer-employees, and the staff now see him in a different light—as one cog in the larger corporate wheel. Mandrake is relieved to be able to delegate management duties to others so he can get back to design work behind his closed office door.

Silikonics Creates an Entity to Attract Outside Investors

Rachid and Chi-Yuan are electronics integrated circuit design consultants to EDA (Electronic Design Automation) companies. They own and work for their own business, Silikonics, LLC, which provides circuit design consulting services.

They formed their LLC for two reasons: taxation and limited liability.

- **Taxation.** Rachid and Chi-Yuan wanted pass-through taxation of business profits (as explained in Chapter 4, co-owned LLCs are taxed as partnerships).

- **Limited liability.** The duo wanted to limit their personal liability under their firm's consulting contracts. Legal disputes in the chip design business can result in large judgments and settlements. Rachid and Chi-Yuan design cutting-edge chips, and they don't want to be liable if one of their chip designs fails.

Now, Rachid and Chi-Yuan want to change their business plan. Instead of providing standard consulting services, they want to develop software code for managing the huge databases employed in chip circuit designs. If successful, their company can patent, then license, its database technology to their current EDA customers. Ultimately, the company might be able to sell its successful EDA database technology to a large EDA firm.

The pair's lawyer and tax adviser both advise converting their LLC to a corporation for the following reasons:

- **Variety of investment choices.** A C corporation can offer a venture capital firm a share in management of the corporation, along with preferred shares, stock warrants, and other corporate-based investment incentives.

- **Stock options, purchase, and bonus plans.** To entice experienced EDA software developers away from larger EDA firms, the corporation can offer unique corporate equity sharing (incentive stock option, restricted stock, and stock purchase) plans, which receive favorable tax treatment under federal and state tax law.

- **Tax-free reorganization.** The C corporation will work best down the road if the business is successful in developing and finding a buyer, because the sale can be structured as part of a tax-free corporate reorganization that merges Silikonics into a larger corporation at minimal tax cost to the corporation and its shareholders (For more information on corporate mergers, see Chapter 9.)

After talking to their lawyer and tax adviser, Rachid and Chi-Yuan decide that forming a C corporation will help them raise capital to fund and grow their new business plan. (See Chapter 8 for more information on converting an LLC to a corporation.)

The Surf Side: From Lunch Counter to LLC to Corporate Franchise

Leila runs a lunch counter business that provides her both a decent income and an escape from the cubicled office environment in which she was once unhappily trapped. She starts her sole proprietorship with a business license, a lease agreement, and little else in the way of formal paperwork.

Business starts out slow but steady, and after a while Leila has a new idea to give the business more appeal: She changes the decor to reflect a tropical motif, installs a salt-water coral reef aquarium facing the lunch counter, adds halogen ceiling lights and light-reflective wall paneling, and renames the business Surf Side. The standard lunch counter fare is augmented with a bouillabaisse soup entrée and a selection of organic salads and fruit juice drinks, and a seafood and sushi dinner menu is added to cater to the after work crowd.

From Sole Proprietorship to Sole-Owner LLC

Leila has her hands full, doing most of the remodeling work and preparing the expanded menu each day. She also takes the time to do a little business research and decides that she should convert from a sole proprietorship to a sole-owner LLC. (See Chapter 6 for more information on this type of conversion.)

Leila wants personal liability protection in case a customer slips and falls, mistakenly alleges that the Surf Side cuisine provoked a gastro-intestinal incident, or brings some other legal claim against her business. She prepares and files articles of organization with the state to form her sole-owner LLC. She also adopts a standard member-managed LLC operating agreement that shows she is the sole owner and capital contributor to her LLC. Leila learns that it looks better to the IRS and a state court if she prepares standard legal paperwork for her LLC, even though she is the only owner.

Although it is now an LLC, Leila's business continues to be treated by the IRS and state as a sole proprietorship, so she continues to report business profits on Schedule C, along with her 1040 individual income tax return.

From One-Owner to Co-Owned LLC

Over the next few years, Surf Side's business continues to swell. Leila decides to seek financing to open a second Surf Side location on the other side of town. Leila's sister, Shannon, has extra cash and a desire to help Leila build up her business. Shannon agrees to invest in Leila's LLC to help fund its expansion but wants no part of the work or worry associated with it.

Leila prepares a new co-owner LLC operating agreement that designates Leila as the sole manager and both Leila and Shannon as the two members (owners) of the LLC. The agreement specifies the capital contributions, profits, voting, and liquidation rights of the co-owners and puts Leila in sole charge of making business decisions for the LLC. Leila knows that her reconstituted LLC will now be treated as a partnership by the IRS and state tax agency, and she hires a small business tax adviser to help her set up a formal financial record-keeping system for her LLC. The adviser will also prepare the year-end partnership tax returns.

From LLC to Corporation

The Surf Side locations are a hit. A newspaper in the nearby capital city features both Surf Side restaurants in an article on tasty eating spots. Patronage increases at both locations, and Leila hires an additional cook and two waiters at each Surf Side to help her handle the rising tide of clientele. Sally, an entrepreneur who represents an investment group, calls Leila to discuss the possibility of investing in the business. Sally asks Leila if she would be interested in franchising other Surf

Sides throughout the state. Sally says her investment group will develop a franchise plan and fund the new operation. Leila would be asked to travel to help set up franchise operations for the first year and would have a well-paid consulting role and a substantial stake in the new venture. Shannon's LLC interest also would be converted to an interest in the new enterprise.

Leila likes the idea of being a consultant and a business stakeholder. Besides, she's feeling overworked managing both Surf Sides, and it would be a welcome relief to have the new venture take over business management. Shannon likes the idea, too; she stands to substantially increase the value of her investment in the Surf Side enterprise if the franchise plan makes a splash. She would also be able to cash out her investment if a publicly traded firm acquires the franchise venture in a stock swap.

The investment group wants a majority managerial role in the franchise operation, plus a comprehensive set of financial controls. Leila and the investment group agree to incorporate the new venture as "Surf Side Franchising, Inc." The corporate business structure is a good fit. Leila will be a director of the new company, along with Sally and another member of the venture capital firm. Leila and Shannon will receive common stock in the corporation. The franchise firm will receive preferred stock with special dividend and liquidation rights, plus stock warrants that the firm can convert to common Surf Side stock within the next five years. Surf Side Franchising, Inc. is formed and hires two seasoned business executives, one as chief executive officer (CEO) and the other as chief financial officer (CFO), to run the new franchise operation. A corporate stock bonus and stock option plan is set up to create incentives for, and reward, new franchisees and their employees. Business begins with the two Surf Sides as the first franchise locations, and Leila gets started setting up other franchise locations throughout the state.

If the new venture is successful, Leila and the investment group can merge the company with a publicly held corporation as part of a tax-free reorganization in exchange for the acquiring company's shares, which can easily be converted to cash on the public market to yield substantial long-term capital gains profits for Leila, Shannon, and the other Surf Side Franchising, Inc., shareholders. ●

State Website Information

The websites described below can provide you with information about the legal and tax rules for forming and operating an LLC or corporation (and other regulated business entities) in your state. We show you how to locate links to each of these websites in your state.

State Business Entity Filing Websites

The state business entity filing office is the office where you file articles (or a similar document) to form a corporation, LLC, limited partnership, or other type of state-regulated business entity. You can also contact this office (either online or by telephone at a number listed on the site) to check the availability of your proposed business entity name and to reserve your name if you wish to do so. State filing office websites typically provide downloadable Articles, name reservation request forms, and the latest corporate and LLC filing fee information.

To find your state's business entity filing office website, go to www .statelocalgov.net. On the left side, under "Select Topic" choose "SOS" for Secretary of State. From your state's secretary of state office, you might need to search the tabs and menus to find the filing or form information you need.

If you don't mind having to provide some information, you can find a direct link to your state's filing office at the website of the National Association of Secretaries of State (NASS) at www.nass.org. Register on the site (for free), then select "Issues," then choose, "Business Services," then select "Corporate Registration" in the left pane, then choose your state to go to the main page for your state's business entity filing office.

State Tax Office Websites

The state tax office website is where you can find state corporate and LLC tax information and forms. Most states collect an annual corporate income or franchise tax, and some states impose an annual LLC tax or fee. To find your state's tax office website, go to the Federation of Tax Administrators website at www.taxadmin.org/fta/link/forms.html, then click on your state.

State Securities Office Websites

The state securities office is the state agency where you can find information and forms for complying with your state's laws regarding selling interests in your corporation, LLC, or other business entity to investors. Most states provide an easy-to-use exemption from state securities registration for the initial issuance of shares by a small corporation to a limited number of investors.

To find your state's securities office website, go to the North American Securities Administrators Association (NASAA) website's "Contact Your Regulator" page at www.nasaa.org/QuickLinks/ContactYourRegulator .cfm, then click on your state. This will lead you to a paragraph that provides contact information for your state's securities agency (agency name, address, and telephone number) followed by a link to their site. Click this link to go to the main page of your state securities office website. ●

Index

NOLO® *Keep Up to Date*

1. Go to Nolo.com/newsletters to sign up for free newsletters and discounts on Nolo products.

   - **Nolo Briefs.** Our monthly email newsletter with great deals and free information.

   - **Nolo's Special Offer.** A monthly newsletter with the biggest Nolo discounts around.

   - **BizBriefs.** Tips and discounts on Nolo products for business owners and managers.

   - **Landlord's Quarterly.** Deals and free tips just for landlords and property managers, too.

2. Don't forget to check for updates at **Nolo.com.** Under "Products," find this book and click "Legal Updates."

Let Us Hear From You

3. Register your Nolo product and give us your feedback at Nolo.com/book-registration.

   - Once you've registered, you qualify for technical support if you have any trouble with a download or CD (though most folks don't).

   - We'll also drop you an email when a new edition of your book is released—and we'll send you a coupon for 15% off your next Nolo.com order!

NOLO® *Catalog*

BUSINESS

Bankruptcy for Small Business Owners	$39.99
Business Buyout Agreements (Book w/CD)	$49.99
Business Loans From Family & Friends: How to Ask, Make It Legal & Make It Work	$29.99
The California Nonprofit Corporation Kit (Binder w/CD)	$69.99
California Workers' Comp: How to Take Charge When You're Injured on the Job	$39.99
The Craft Artist's Legal Guide (Book w/CD)	$39.99
The Complete Guide to Buying a Business (Book w/CD)	$24.99
The Complete Guide to Selling a Business (Book w/CD)	$34.99
Consultant & Independent Contractor Agreements (Book w/CD)	$34.99
The Corporate Records Handbook (Book w/CD)	$69.99
Create Your Own Employee Handbook (Book w/CD)	$49.99
Dealing With Problem Employees	$49.99
Deduct It! Lower Your Small Business Taxes	$34.99
The eBay Business Start-Up Kit (Book w/CD)	$24.99
Effective Fundraising for Nonprofits	$24.99
The Employer's Legal Handbook	$49.99
The Essential Guide to Family & Medical Leave (Book w/CD)	$49.99
The Essential Guide to Federal Employment Laws	$44.99
The Essential Guide to Handling Workplace Discrimination & Harassment	$39.99
The Essential Guide to Workplace Investigations (Book w/CD)	$44.99
Every Nonprofit's Guide to Publishing	$29.99
Every Nonprofit's Tax Guide	$34.99
Form a Partnership (Book w/CD)	$39.99
Form Your Own Limited Liability Company (Book w/CD)	$44.99
Healthy Employees, Healthy Business	$29.99
Hiring Your First Employee: A Step-by-Step Guide	$24.99
Home Business Tax Deductions: Keep What You Earn	$34.99
How to Form a Nonprofit Corporation (Book w/CD)—National Edition	$49.99
How to Form a Nonprofit Corporation in California (Book w/CD)	$49.99
How to Form Your Own California Corporation (Binder w/CD)	$39.99
How to Form Your Own California Corporation (Book w/CD)	$39.99
How to Run a Thriving Business: Strategies for Success & Satisfaction	$19.99
How to Write a Business Plan (Book w/CD)	$34.99
Incorporate Your Business (Book w/CD)—National Edition	$49.99
The Job Description Handbook (Book w/CD)	$29.99
Legal Guide for Starting & Running a Small Business	$39.99
Legal Forms for Starting & Running a Small Business (Book w/CD)	$29.99
LLC or Corporation?	$24.99
The Manager's Legal Handbook	$49.99
Marketing Without Advertising	$20.00
Music Law: How to Run Your Band's Business (Book w/CD)	$39.99
Negotiate the Best Lease for Your Business	$24.99
Nolo's Crash Course in Small Business Basics (Audiobook on 5 CDs)	$34.99
Nolo's Quick LLC	$29.99

Order 24 hours a day at Nolo.com or call 800-728-3555

Nonprofit Meetings, Minutes & Records (Book w/CD)..$39.99
The Performance Appraisal Handbook (Book w/CD)..$29.99
The Progressive Discipline Handbook (Book w/CD)..$34.99
Retire—And Start Your Own Business (Book w/CD)..$24.99
Running a Side Business: How to Create a Second Income $21.99
Save Your Small Business: 10 Crucial Strategies to Survive Hard Times or Close Down & Move On $29.99
Small Business in Paradise: Working for Yourself in a Place You Love $19.99
The Small Business Start-Up Kit (Book w/CD)—National Edition..$29.99
The Small Business Start-Up Kit for California (Book w/CD) $29.99
Smart Policies for Workplace Technologies: Email, Blogs, Cell Phones & More (Book w/CD) $29.99
Starting & Building a Nonprofit: A Practical Guide (Book w/CD)..$29.99
Starting & Running a Successful Newsletter or Magazine..$29.99
Tax Deductions for Professionals $39.99
Tax Savvy for Small Business $39.99
The Women's Small Business Start-Up Kit (Book w/CD)..$29.99
The Work From Home Handbook $19.99
Working for Yourself: Law & Taxes for Independent Contractors, Freelancers & Consultants $39.99
Working With Independent Contractors (Book w/CD) $34.99
Your Limited Liability Company (Book w/CD) $49.99
Your Rights in the Workplace..$29.99

CONSUMER
How to Win Your Personal Injury Claim..$34.99
The Judge Who Hated Red Nail Polish & Other Crazy but True Stories of Law and Lawyers $19.99
Nolo's Encyclopedia of Everyday Law..$29.99
Nolo's Guide to California Law $34.99
Nolo's Plain-English Law Dictionary $29.99
The Sharing Solution: How to Save Money, Simplify Your Life & Build Community $24.99
Your Little Legal Companion $9.95

ESTATE PLANNING & PROBATE
8 Ways to Avoid Probate $21.99
Estate Planning Basics..$24.99
Estate Planning for Blended Families: Providing for Your Spouse & Children in a Second Marriage $34.99
The Executor's Guide: Settling a Loved One's Estate or Trust..$39.99
Get It Together: Organize Your Records So Your Family Won't Have To (Book w/CD) $21.99
How to Probate an Estate in California $49.99
Living Wills & Powers of Attorney for California..$29.99
Make Your Own Living Trust (Book w/CD) $39.99
The Mom's Guide to Wills & Estate Planning $21.99
Plan Your Estate..$44.99
Quick & Legal Will Book (Book w/CD)..$21.99
Quicken Willmaker Plus (Book and Software) $49.99
Special Needs Trusts: Protect Your Child's Financial Future (Book w/CD) $34.99
The Trustee's Legal Companion $39.99

FAMILY MATTERS
Always Dad: Being a Great Father During & After a Divorce..$16.99
Building a Parenting Agreement That Works $24.99
The Complete IEP Guide: How to Advocate for Your Special Ed Child $34.99
Divorce After 50..$29.99
Divorce & Money: How to Make the Best Financial Decisions During Divorce $34.99

Divorce Without Court: A Guide to Mediation & Collaborative Divorce $34.99
Every Dog's Legal Guide: A Must-Have for Your Owner $19.99
Get It Together: Organize Your Records So Your Family Doesn't Have To (Book w/CD)......................... $21.99
The Guardianship Book for California $44.99
A Judge's Guide to Divorce (Book w/CD) $24.99
A Legal Guide for Lesbian & Gay Couples (Book w/CD) $34.99
Living Together: A Legal Guide for Unmarried Couples (Book w/CD) $34.99
Making It Legal: A Guide to Same-Sex Marriage, Domestic Partnerships & Civil Unions $29.99
Nannies & Au Pairs: Hiring In-Home Childcare $19.99
Nolo's Essential Guide to Divorce $24.99
Nolo's IEP Guide: Learning Disabilities $34.99
Parent Savvy $19.99
Prenuptial Agreements (Book w/CD) $34.99

GOING TO COURT
Beat Your Ticket: Go to Court & Win—National Edition $21.99
The Criminal Law Handbook: Know Your Rights, Survive the System $39.99
Everybody's Guide to Small Claims Court—National Edition... $29.99
Everybody's Guide to Small Claims Court in California $29.99
Fight Your Ticket & Win in California... $29.99
How to Change Your Name in California (Book w/CD).. $34.99
Legal Research: How to Find & Understand the Law $49.99
Nolo's Deposition Handbook.. $34.99
Represent Yourself in Court: How to Prepare & Try a Winning Case $39.99
Win Your Lawsuit: A Judge's Guide to Representing Yourself in California Superior Court $39.99

HOMEOWNERS, LANDLORDS & TENANTS
Buying a Second Home (Book w/CD) $24.99
The California Landlord's Law Book: Evictions (Book w/CD).. $44.99
The California Landlord's Law Book: Rights & Responsibilities (Book w/CD) $44.99
California Tenants' Rights $29.99
Deeds for California Real Estate $27.99
The Essential Guide for First-Time Homeowners $19.99
Every Landlord's Guide to Finding Great Tenants (Book w/CD) $24.99
Every Landlord's Legal Guide (Book w/CD) $44.99
Every Landlord's Property Protection Guide (Book w/CD) $29.99
Every Landlord's Tax Deduction Guide $39.99
Every Tenant's Legal Guide... $34.99
First-Time Landlord: Your Guide to Renting Out a Single-Family Home.. $19.99
For Sale by Owner in California (Book w/CD) $29.99
The Foreclosure Survival Guide $24.99
Leases & Rental Agreements (Book w/CD) $29.99
Neighbor Law: Fences, Trees, Boundaries & Noise $29.99
Nolo's Essential Guide to Buying Your First Home (Book w/CD) $24.99
Renters' Rights: The Basics $24.99
Saving the Family Cottage: A Guide to Succession Planning for Your Cottage, Cabin, Camp or
   Vacation Home.. $29.99
Selling Your House in a Tough Market: 10 Strategies That Work... $24.99

IMMIGRATION
Becoming a U.S. Citizen: A Guide to the Law, Exam & Interview $24.99
Fiancé & Marriage Visas.. $34.99

NOLO® *Online Legal Forms*

Nolo offers a large library of legal solutions and forms, created by Nolo's in-house legal staff. These reliable documents can be prepared in minutes.

Create a Document

- **Incorporation.** Incorporate your business in any state.
- **LLC Formations.** Gain asset protection and pass-through tax status in any state.
- **Wills.** Nolo has helped people make over 2 million wills. Is it time to make or revise yours?
- **Living Trust (avoid probate).** Plan now to save your family the cost, delays, and hassle of probate.
- **Trademark.** Protect the name of your business or product.
- **Provisional Patent.** Preserve your rights under patent law and claim "patent pending" status.

Download a Legal Form

Nolo.com has hundreds of top quality legal forms available for download—bills of sale, promissory notes, nondisclosure agreements, LLC operating agreements, corporate minutes, commercial lease and sublease, motor vehicle bill of sale, consignment agreements and many, many more.

Review Your Documents

Many lawyers in Nolo's consumer-friendly lawyer directory will review Nolo documents for a very reasonable fee. Check their detailed profiles at **Nolo.com/lawyers**.

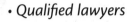

NOLO® *Lawyer Directory*

Find a Business Attorney

- *Qualified lawyers*
- *In-depth profiles*
- *A pledge of respectful service*

When you want help with your small business, you don't want just any lawyer—you want an expert in the field, who can give you up-to-the-minute advice. You need a lawyer who has the experience and knowledge to answer your questions about protecting your personal assets, hiring and firing employees, drafting contracts, protecting your name and trademarks and a dozen other common business concerns.

Nolo's Lawyer Directory is unique because it provides an extensive profile of every lawyer. You'll learn about not only each lawyer's education, professional history, legal specialties, credentials and fees, but also about their philosophy of practicing law and how they like to work with clients.

All lawyers listed in Nolo's directory are in good standing with their state bar association. Many will review Nolo documents, such as a will or living trust, for a fixed fee. They all pledge to work diligently and respectfully with clients—communicating regularly, providing a written agreement about how legal matters will be handled, sending clear and detailed bills, and more.

www.nolo.com